# THE CASE OF

# MOTHER

A JACK BURTON MURDER MYSTERY

WRITTEN BY: WILLIAM ELLIOTT KERN

STORY BY: WILLIAM ELLIOTT KERN

COPYRIGHT@JANUARY 30, 2023

**CHAPTER ONE**


**BENNY'S BAR AND GRILL**


"Another round on table four." Benny yelled to his waitress.

"Hey Benny, how about some music from your Jute Box....you got Elvis on your list of songs?"  Darlene sighed..."Elvis makes me C...." Jack Burton interrupted the blonde bomb shell sitting at the bar.

The Bar and Grill was hopping...over loaded with drunk customers and not enough chairs for everyone to sit on.  The ancient Jute Box was cranked up so loud that the building was shaking.  The walls of the Bar and Grill were digging Elvis's big hits....  "You ain't nothin but a hound dog was number one."

Everyone inside Bennys Bar were regulars.  Tonight, the special menu was Mexican food, chips and American Whiskey. The Women were looking for hook ups for the night, using the private rooms upstairs.

The Men were bragging about the Raiders game, hoping that the Steelers would take the Super Bowl.

"Dude...we're running out a Sud's and Whiskey.  Tuesday looked a bit lost when her boyfriend entered the Bar and Grill, his clothes covered in Blood, his face crushed by a homeless dude named Oscar.

Oscar was a regular at Bennys Bar pledging never to drink booze again. This pledge of Oscar's was renewed Dailey. "Hey guys, you all met Oscar, ahh...no I'm Oscar.  The dude I whipped in your parking lot, was for trying to take my bottle...thought you all might help this asshole...I was rough with him for trying to steal my stuff.

"Rough...geez, you knocked his teeth out and looks like you broke his jaw.  Tuesday...call the paramedics." Jack sighed.

" This guy has lost way too much blood."  Benny sighed, yelling for the patrons to let the paramedic's pass through the crowd to help the man. "You nearly killed this guy...." Manny sighed.  "You're 86 shit head. Get outa my Bar."

After the medics attended to the half dead man, Benny took to the mic to wake up the 70 or so customers for some wild drinking and exotic-dancing.

"Hey, hey, hey, It's my Birthday." Benny turned on the mic and woke up the boozers with a song of "Happy Birthday to himself"... Most of the patrons' were already drunk, trying to sing with Benny,  mumbling the words to Happy, "firthday."

Jimmy Three Fingers, Jack's number one man, entered the Bar and Grill looking for Jack. Jimmy's face was swollen, his clothes ripped and his shoes gone.

The noise inside the Bar was drowning out Jimmys words.  "Benny, let me use the mic for a second, will ya?"  Jimmy took the mic, clicked the volume to 10 and yelled for jack to meet with him outside, pronto."  Jimmy Returned the mic to Benny and left the Bar waiting for jack to meet him in the parking lot.

"Dude, you look like shit...what happened to you?" Jack sighed, sipping a glass of Whiskey with a beer chaser. Jack and Jimmy stood in the Parking lot of Bennys Bar and Grill talking, then got in Jimmy's Corolla and closed the doors.

"Dude...we got problems dude."  Jimmy sighed.

"Alright...alright...so what's got your nuts?"  Jack downed his glass of Whiskey, working on the beer chaser.

"We gotta a new case...Manny Gonzales wants us at the precinct pronto for the details."

"Jimmy boy, we're celebrating Bennys 50th. It's rude to leave the Bar without explaining to Benny what's happening, right?"

"No time. Sarg has bodies comin outa his ass...He needs us to handle a super sensitive case and find the killer or killers who are on rampage killing everyone and anyone, throughout the city."

"Is the media involved yet?"  Jack sighed, trying to finish his drink.
"Not yet...we gotta investigate this mess before the media finds out about the slaughters.  The city is on high alert thanks to Manny."

"Okay bud, but you need to take a shower, change your clothes while I say goodbye and happy Birthday to Benny."  Jack was already tipsy from the Whiskey and beer.

"Jack, no time. Manny said the killer or killers are aliens...you know...from outer space dude."  Jimmy grabbed Jack's arm, seat belting him inside his corolla.   Jack and Jimmy headed direct to the Police Precinct, passing numerous dead bodies lying on the roadside, rotting.

"Dude, you smell like a Dog.  What did you fall into, a pile of dog shit?" Jack sighed.

"Shut up Jack....I'm not happy about my circumstances either."  Jimmy sighed.

"So, what happened to you?" Jack looked at Jimmy with dismay.

"A dog...?"  Jimmy sighed.

"A Dog...what does that mean?"  Jack smiled, laughing privately inside his mind.

"I left the Precinct when a giant dog attacked me.  At least I think it was a Dog.  You happy now?  Come on, Manny is waiting for us." Jimmy coughed, choking from the rancid animal smell of dog shit on his clothes.

"I'll walk to the Precinct. Meet you there." Jack looked at Jimmy, shaking his head.

"Get back inside the damn car. We got murders cropping up all over the city. Manny's waiting for us." Jimmy was adamant, let alone, pissed at Jack for making an joke of Jimmy's mishap with the Dog.

"Okay...you got a mask I can wear to keep the smell of your clothes from gagging me.  Dude, I'm gonna puke."  Jack was being a dick. Jimmy Three Fingers was in no mode for Jacks asshole remarks.

The two retired cops drove to the Pasadena Police Precinct to meet with Sargent Manny Gonzales.

"Jimmy, where we goin...the Precinct is in the other direction."  Jack frowned, confused.

"Jack, I'm not in control of my car.  Something or someone else has control of my car. I can't control the Corolla."  Jimmy was in a panic and Jack was falling asleep from the booze, laying back in the front passenger seat of Jimmy's Corolla.

"Huh..." Jimmy elbowed Jack in his gut.  "Wake up bro, we're in trouble. I can't Steer the car."

"Keep trying. Use your brakes..."  Jack was trying to keep his eyes opened, fighting the power of the Whiskey closing his mind.

"We're not stopping Bro. Worse yet, my Corolla is rising above the Street. We're floating in mid-air."  Jimmy looked out the driver's side window.  Jack was now awake, looking out the passenger side window, hovering some 50 feet above the roadway, below.

"Any idea what's happening to us Jimmy Boy?"  Jack frowned, his head hanging out his window, puking his guts out.

Jimmy and his Corolla were ascending higher and higher into the clouds above them, without stopping.

"I got nothin Jack. I'm thinking we're inside of some kinda tornado or something..." Jimmy sighed.  Jack, wake up and wipe your mouth from the puke."

"Great...so, when the Tornado drops us from about 100 feet above the ground below." Jack interrupted Jimmy's thought.

"Hold that thought. We're starting to return to civilization below. Your Corolla is slowly dropping us back down to the street below us." Jack smiled.  "Now...let's hope this Tornado drops us slowly to the ground?" Jack was shaken, not stirred.

"We're not dropping downward Jack. We're moving forward.  I don't think we're inside of a Tornado."  Jimmy sighed. "We're not dropping lower or going higher...it's like we're in limbo, moving in a forward direction, no ups or downs."

"Okay. Good...then let's sit back and see who's taking us for a ride." Jack kept looking out his window, wishing he brought a bottle of Whiskey with him. No such luck.

"Ah...look out the windshield..." Jack Yelled at Jimmy.

"Geeze...is that some kind of a Plane?" Jimmy sighed.

"Looks like an outhouse to me. The door is opening and it's way too small for your corolla to pass through." Jack shook his head.  "Dude, we're not gonna pass through this Cube or whatever it is. We're gonna crash."

"It looks like a shitter...a damn outhouse...what is this thing?  Okay Jack...hang on...the door to this floating outhouse is opening.  We're headed right to it."

Jack pulled down on his seat belt tightening the strap. Jimmy  hunkered down on the floor of the Corolla.  Jimmy's car was about to crash into a floating outhouse.

The Corolla easily passed through the open door of the floating house, with the door closing behind them, including the Corolla.

"We're still floating right?"  Jack sighed.

"Hell, if I know...I think we're caught inside this thing.  I think we just entered a floating Shitter...or..." Jack interrupted his friend.

"Nope...we just entered some kind of a rat-tailed Space Ship."  Jack sighed.

"So, what's a Rat-Tailed Space Ship doing floating 100 feet above the clouds in our sky?" Jimmy coughed.  "Jack, this garage thing is beginning to move...with us inside of it...whoa...like we're moving at light speed.   Hang on dude."

The garage like Space Ship disappeared in the clouds overhead the City of Pasadena.  Jimmy and Jack, we're seat-belted inside the Corolla, passing a compliment of Stars, Asteroids, and space junk from voided Satellites.

"Hey, maybe we just met the thing that Manny Gonzales wanted us to investigate.  I think this thing floating in space is dead." Jimmy sighed. At least it's not moving."

"So why the Hollywood Movie.  We're being swallowed up inside this crate." Jack, was having a hard time breathing.

"Dude...was this red button on my dash board before?"  Jimmy sighed.

"I can't breathe Jimbo...push the Blue button."  Jack was struggling to breathe.

"Red Button...this thing wasn't on my dash before.  My car is being re-arranged into some kind of a vehicle or room.  Jimmy pushed the red button and the Corolla's air conditioning began spewing relief throughout the Car.

"Dude, can you breathe better now?"  Jimmy looked at Jacks purple colored Face.

"Yeah...I'm getting Air to breathe...Jack sighed. "I told you to push the blue button, not the red button."

"Whatever we're inside of is now supplying air for us to breathe" Jack coughed, taking deep breaths.

"Dude, it's the air conditioning in your car."  Jack frowned.

"I don't have air conditioning in my car.  It's something else dude."

**CHAPTER 2**


**SPACE**


"So, where are we Dude?"  Jimmy sighed. "There's no sign of anything except, black, empty, space, Jack."

"Right...but I can breathe now. We're not inside the Corolla any longer. So, where's your car Jimmy?"  Jack looked around seeing only darkness.

The two friends were inside of a six-sided square box, seemly going in an upward direction to the Stars.

"Dude, we've been hijacked." Jimmy looked at Jack.

"You had to use my name to tell me we're in deep shit?" Jack sighed. "Jimbo, when your eyes adjust to the dark, take a look around this six-sided space ship.  See if there's a door for us to get outa here, and let's find out what happened to your car."

"Jack...we're flying somewhere over the rainbow. Like we're in deep space Dude."  Jimmy sighed.

"How do you know that?  Deep Space Dude shit.  We're inside this square box, right?" Jack was feeling better, able to breathe.

"It takes time to leave Earth and jump into Deep Space. Any idea what's happening to us?" Jack was searching the walls and floor for an escape route. Without success.

"Okay, so where's my Corolla?  Did you see it disappear?  Jack, we've been unconscious for a time...maybe a long time?"  Jimmy sighed. "This box is vibrating. Which means we're still moving."

"You're right Jimbo.  Keep looking for an exit..." Jack ordered jimmy to continue searching the walls, the floor, the ceiling, for some sort of power source propelling the Box the two Detectives were captive inside of.

After a few minutes, Jimmy returned to Jacks side, where he found Jack lying on the floor of the crate like Space Ship, unconscious.

"Dude...wake up...Jack...can you hear me?"  Jimmy sighed.

"Huh, what...Jimbo?  where are we?"  Jack coughed, struggling again for air to breathe.

"Jack....we're still inside some kind of a space ship?"  Jimmy's eyes had finally adjusted to the darkness. "Bro, there's a door knob on one of the walls.  Let's see if the knob will open a door for us to escape?" Jimmy was hopeful.

"Sure...but slowly...there might be dark space on the other side of this door."  Jack was trying to stand up. "Here, let me help you." Jimmy sighed.

 "Jimmy, turn the knob on this door... hopefully, it's a possible escape route for us." Jack was positive.

The two mates got to the knob, twisted it open, exposing them to a passage way.  A long hall-way was on the other side of the Door, so long, that the two friends could not see an end to it.

"At least we have light and Air...let's continue forward...maybe we'll meet up with the owner of this so-called Crate we're held captive inside of." Jack was hopeful and feeling a bit normal again.

The two continued walking through the hallway. There are lights in the ceiling of the hall, with multiple doors along the way to a possible exit.

"Dude, I can hear sounds. Sounds of people talking.  Can you hear it too?" Jack asked Jimmy.

"Yeah, I can hear a lot of people talking from inside one of the doors. Sounds like a party is happening.  You think we should try and open the door and see what' going on...inside?" Jimmy was anxious to find others inside this make shift space ship.

"You wanna try to open the door where the sounds are coming from. See who's on the other side? Maybe whoever is inside this tin can, will explain what's going on here, right?" Jack looked at Jimmy, hopeful of getting answers to what's happening to the two friends.

"You first..." Jack removed his 9mm, just in case a snag exposed itself.

"Got it. The sounds are louder behind this door.  You really want me to open the door?  What if there's Aliens on the other side of the door. Jack, what if the Aliens are cannibals?"  Jimmy looked at Jack, while trying to hide his fear of the unknown.

"Don't worry Jimbo, you're too skinny for anyone to eat, especially by a hungry Alien. Help me open the door."  Jack sighed.

Jack and Jimmy stood infront of the door where the party sounds were coming from, contemplating to knock on the door or to just open the door and see what was on the other side.

"You ready?" Jack asked Jimmy.

"No, I don't want to be some Alien's meal Jack...you open the door and I'll follow you...okay?" Jimmy sighed.

Before the two Detectives could open this hopeful escape route, the door began opening on its own.

Both men were silent while watching the door opening.

"Ah shit..." Jack and Jimmy sighed in unison. "What the hell is that thing staring at us?" Jimmy was sickened at the sight of an Alien Blob looking at them, hunger in its eyes.

"Hum...Jimbo, we can't go back. So, take a deep breath...we got no more options." Jack coughed. "Run..."

 Inside of the opened door was a brash, bulbous Slug, dripping in slime, licking its chops as the two Humans looked at the creature.

Jimmy and Jack side stepped the Giant Alien slug, running past the creature to the other side of the room.

"Dude, we die here or we make it to the door beyond the Slug and make our way out of this maze of shit." Jack sighed.

Jack and Jimmy ran pasted the Slug to the door at the other side of this room. The Giant Slug slowly turned its bulbous body towards the two meaty humans, slithering towards the second locked door in the room, slime dripping from its toothless mouth.

"There is no way out of my room...there is no place to hide...come to me NOW and I will let you die in glory...come to me...I am hungry."  The Slimed Creature coughed up slime from its mouth.

The giant Slug was imagining the consumption of the two Humans.  Jack and Jimmy began searching the room they were caught inside of, hoping to find a way to escape their confines.

Jack yelled for Jimmy...."Follow me, Jimmy. Take my hand...hurry Jimbo...I found a way out a here."

Jack rolled over in his bed, mumbling about an Alien Slug, slime dripping monster, hoping to ingest the two bodies of Jack and Jimmy Three Fingers.

Jimmy and Benny ran upstairs to Jacks room, knocking on his door.  Jack was fighting an invisible foe who was inside his mind.  Jimmy and Benny slammed opened the Bedroom door to Jacks room, finding Jack laying on the floor of his room, engulfed in slime.

"Jack, what happened to you...?"  Benny sighed.  "Dude, you're covered in some slimy shit, bro."

"Jack, you know better than to get drunk and go to bed.  Every fricken time you do this, you wind up in the throes of some Alien Monster trying to consume you and anyone else that exists in your Dream World." Jimmy shook his head in dismay.

Jimmy bent over, trying to get Jack's Slime infested body up off the floor and into his bathroom for a shower.

"Jimmy....this dream was way too real...look at me.  I'm covered in slime."  Jack sighed. "How is this possible?"

"No Jack... your covered in sweat, mixed with Whiskey Bro....take a shower, we need to go downtown and meet with Manny Gonzales. We got troubles on the Streets.  Wash your ass, change your clothes and let's go to the Precinct." Jimmy was adamant.

**CHAPTER 3**

**PASADENA POLICE PRECINCT**

Jimmy called on Benny to get Jack ready for a critical meeting with Sargent Manny Gonzales of the Pasadena Police Department.

"Jack, take a shower...dude you stink like a dead Rat."  Jimmy coughed.

Jimmy called Sargent Manny Gonzales to let him know that he and Jack will be at the Precinct in an hour or so.

"Why we going to the Precinct?"  Jack was still in a daze, passing in and out of the dream state that took him into a world that few have ever experienced.  Jack was allowed to see his future death in living color.

Jack finished his well needed Shower, dressed and headed downstairs to meet with Jimmy.

"Hey Jack, Jimmy is waiting for you in his Corolla.  You okay now to travel to the meeting with the Sarge?"  Benny was hoping for a positive response from Jack.

"Yeah...I'm okay now. The shower woke me up. Thanks Benny."  Jack opened his cell phone and placed a call to Sargent Gonzales.

"I'll be there in half an hour...okay Manny?" Jack was looking for his bottle of Whiskey, getting ready to meet with Jimmy in the parking lot.

"Boss, no more booze.  You gotta meeting with Manny, sober up.  You need to be ready for the meeting buddy."  Benny warned Jack.

"Dude.  What happened to you?  You look like a dead man walking Jack. you had the same dream again...the "SLUG.""

"I don't understand Benny. What's happening to me? My head is on fire and my skin is burning flames." Jack sighed.  "Anyhow. What do you want?"

"Jimmy is waiting for you outside.  You need to get to the Corolla." Benny Scoffed.

"Jack, you're losing it again Bro.  Jimmy's outside waiting for you...okay?" Benny scoffed. "Take a breath and go outside ...now." Jack was hearing the same comments over and over again, replayed in his mind.

"Hey, slow down bud.  I'm trying to gather my thoughts.  Jimmy can wait a few seconds...okay Benny?" Jack seemed more coherent than before.

"Yeah, sure thing Jack.  Sorry to push you."  Benny coughed. "Just worried about you...okay?"

"Thanks Bud.  Can you help me put on my coat?  It's freezing outside." Jack was fighting to maintain his conscious state and not pass out on the floor infront of Benny.

"Yeah, sure thing Pal. Come here and take a seat.  I'll get your coat." Benny ran upstairs to Jacks room to get his coat.

Benny returned with Jacks coat, gun and hat.

Jimmy entered the Bar in a rage, yelling at Jack to get up and follow him to the parking lot.

"Manny is having a fit...he needs us in the Precinct for a meeting with his Captain." Jimmy sighed. "Jack, you okay...we need to go to the Precinct to meet with Manny and his team an hour ago."

"So, what's the hurry...why are you always repeating the conversation to me. Geeze Jimbo...I'm in pain dude. You better go without me." Jack sat down at one of Benny's cocktail tables waving for Benny to bring him a glass and a bottle of Whiskey.

"No booze JACKSON....GET YOUR SORRY ASS UP AND COME WITH ME TO THE COROLLA. THE WHOLE PASADENA POLICE DEPARTMENT IS WAITING FOR THE AMAZING JACK BURTON. Now let's hit the road to the Precinct...okay buddy?"

Jack stood up, wobbled a bit, then straighten his walk and left the bar to Jimmy's Corolla.

A 15-minute drive to the Pasadena Police Department was finally underway. Jimmy's Corolla was on its proverbial last leg and was chugging and coughing its way to the Precinct.

"Jack, shape up. We got a meeting with the big wigs." Jimmy was filling Jack in about the upcoming meeting with the hacks running the Precinct.

"So, what's the urgency Jimbo....I'm having a hard time focusing on you. Sorry, but today is not one of my best...okay?" Jack sighed.

"Don't worry old friend...I'm with you all the way. Ah, we're here at the Precinct." Jimmy pulled his Corolla into a parking space and escorted jack through the front doors of the Precinct.

"Hey Burton, follow me to the conference room. The big wigs are waiting for you and Jimmy." The Desk Sargent directed the two Detectives. "We got bodies all over town, and their disappearing like pancakes."

"Hey Jack, hurry up...the meeting is underway." Manny Gonzales directed Jack and Jimmy to the war room.

"Burton...about time you got here. Take a seat. We got something real bad going on here in the Los Angeles basin, and unfortunately, you and your sidekick here are the only one with Alien experience." Captain Foster frowned, not excited about using Burton on a case as serious as an Alien Invasion.

"So, what's up Cap?" Jack was insolent after hearing the Police Captain upset that a retired drunk Detective was the only one the Captain could use to solve this secret and highly classified Top Secret mission.

"Sargent Gonzales will bring you both up to date on the multiple deaths. I suggest you two immediately run over to the Coroners Lab and take a look at the bodies that were retrieved. it's gonna be an eye opener Burton...Remember...Top Secret."

The captain left the room with the other Detectives, the Mayor of the City, and a handful of loser private dick's, heading up the Scorpion Squad.

Jack, Jimmy, Manny and the Scorpion Squad were left in private session, inside the War Room, discussing what had happened and what needed to be done...pronto.

## CHAPTER 4


## THE FIRST ENCOUNTER


"Look, we don't need Old Man Burton and his 3-man crew to lead this investigation.  The Scorpion Squad will wrap up this security issue, take out the losers who are on a killing spree, kill those leaders as Traitors to the States."  Johnson Burns espoused his opinion against using the Burton Crew.  "No offense Jack, but you're used and abused bud.  In other words, you and your friends will get in our way to end the killings and resume the peace in the Los Angeles Basin.

"Look pal, we've been on the front lines of eliminating Hell and guys like you with a big mouth.  Your so-called Scorpion Squad has no idea what you're getting into."  Jack sighed.

"Look suds...let the professionals do the job...you can go back to your customers at the Bar and Grill and drink your Whiskey. The Scorpion Squad will eliminate whoever it is killing innocents here in the Los Angeles Basin...Okay?' Johnson Burns chided Jack and Jimmy with insults and demeaning comments.

"From the intel presented to us, you and your Scorpions will be eliminated at your first encounter.  The intel is way beyond bullets Burns.  Your team will be dissolved the minute you advance against the killers." Jimmy looked at the asshole Leader of the Scorpion Squad." smirking at Manny Gonzales.

"Manny, these guys have no idea what their stepping into...They'll be eliminated at their first assault against the "SLUG." Jimmy turned his head looking at Jack..."You agree Jack?"

"Sargent Gonzales, let the Scorpions handle this case.  We're equipped with all the high tec weaponry needed to kill this Alien or Aliens." Burn's frowned at Jack and Benny.

"Look, intel shows that the SLUG'S are intelligent Creatures that came from the depths of the Earth.  The creatures are on the move.  The creatures have come topside, ravaging Humans indiscriminately, consuming every life form in their path." Sargent Manny Gonzales sighed.

"We have already lost over a 100 Officers and more than 1000 innocents consumed by the creatures.  We don't have time for a mistake...we need to send the SLUG'S back inside the Earth forever. " Manny Gongales sighed, looking at the Scorpion Boss, then Jack and Jimmy Three Fingers.

"Your intel didn't show that Aliens came from inside the Earth.  So, we're actually talking about Earthly Aliens, not Aliens from Space?  My team have eliminated Aliens in the past.  Your intel says the Creatures have made their way to the surface of our Planet in the thousands, true?"  Burns sighed.  "Has the U.S. Military confronted these creatures from inside the Earth Sargent?"

"Like I said Burns, over 100 officers have disappeared.  We believe the creatures have taken our Officers down, inside the Earth's crust, as food, sustenance.  We believe that The SLUG'S like the taste of Human Meat.  Remember Burns, over a 1000 people have disappeared from the surface of the Earth, beyond those 100 Cops." Sargent Gonzales was lost for words.

"So, Manny.  Pasadena is the only location where Innocents and your Cops have disappeared...probably into the confines of the Earth's Crust, Right?"  Jack looked at Jimmy, a frown on his face.

"Yeah...Jack, we have proof that something has emerged from the depths of the Earth, attacked our cops and gathered over a thousand innocents from the streets.  My Cops and over 1000 local residents disappeared into an opening in the Earth, just outside of the Pasadena City limits."  Manny sighed, wishing that the investigation would get underway before more Residents disappear.

"Jack, some Residents say they saw giant creatures entering a hole in the asphalt road, just outside of the City Limits of Pasadena, dumping bodies of My Cop's and some Residents into this hole."  Manny sighed.

"This is bullshit...it's impossible for life to exist inside the confines of the Earth.  It's impossible, what kind of a joke are you playing."  Burns was pissed.  "You want Burton to deal with the Alien creatures existing inside the Earth, fine, let him and his losers do the job....We're out."  The Scorpion Leader left the Precinct laughing.

"Why's the guy laughing?" Jimmy sighed.

"Scared?  Jimbo....the big mouth, muscle bound fool has no idea what's attacking the Los Angeles Basin."  Jack and jimmy kept talking with Manny Gonzales as the Scorpion Boys took their leave from the Precinct.

"So, you and your team still willing to investigate this invasion and squash Aliens." Manny asked Jimmy and Jack?

"Manny, you have a location where the hole exists?" Jimmy asked the Sargent.

"Yeah...kinda...."  Manny sighed.

"Well, yes, or no?"  Jack sighed.

"Jack, the hole keeps moving.  Small Buildings, School Houses, Restaurants...you know what I mean... places are being sucked inside the Earth, disappearing below ground.

"Manny, we're told by the Scorpion Gang that something had come up from the Earth, from thousands of feet below the Earth's Crust, according to our radar experts."  Manny was cautious not telling Jack and Jimmy more until they agreed to take the "CASE of THE INVASION OF THE SLUG'S."

## CHAPTER 5

## THE CORONERS LAB

" Manny, do you guys have a body?' Jack asked the Sargent of the Pasadena Police Department.

"Kinda. I mean, we have a body but it's not like anything you guys have ever seen before." Manny frowned.

"So, let's go to the Coroners Lab and see what's been killing our Residents." Jimmy was anxious to get started on the Case.

"Sure. I'll set up a meeting." Manny sighed.

"Bullshit...there's no time for a meeting. Call the Coroner and tell him we're on the way to see the body, post haste." Jack and Jimmy headed to the Corolla and took off to visit the Coroners Lab.

"Jimbo, we need to see what we're getting ourselves into here. The coroner sounds skeptible to allow us inside his Lab to get a look at the dead killer." Jack was anxious to get started on the Case.

Jack and Jimmy Three Fingers finally arrived at the Coroners Lab to get a look at the only body that had been captured. The Body was evidently discovered in one of the open holes in "Bloom's Park."

"Jack, the door to the Coroners Lab is locked." Jimmy was confused. "Doesn't look like anyone is working here...today."

"Keep knocking Jimmy until the Bastard opens up.  We gotta view this body to see what we're facing here." Jack sighed. "Keep knocking.  I'll go around to the back side of the Lab and see if the back door is opened."

Jack left Jimmy knocking at the front door of the Coroners Lab, while he walked to the back door of the building, finding the door unlocked.

Jack entered the Lab, heading to the front door of the Lab to let Jimmy get inside.

"Geeze, the Back door was unlocked?  Did you see anyone inside when you entered the building?" Jimmy asked Jack.

"Nothin man...no one is inside this Lab.  There's something strange though Jim...there's a hole in the floor and it looks like it's super deep." Jack told Jimmy to follow him to the center of the Lab where the giant hole was found.  "Jim, turn on the lights.  You have your flash light on you?"

"Jimmy stood on the edge of the hole in the floor, teetering back and forth, trying to spot if someone or something was inside the hole. "Dude, the hole looks endless. Let's drop something down the hole and see how deep it goes?" Jimmy thought he saw movement in the darkness of the hole below the floor of the Lab.

Jack looked around the room after the lights of the Laboratory were turned on by Jimmy.  "Find me something to drop down inside the opening Jimbo and start counting from 1 to infinity." Jack smiled at his friend.

"Jack, I gotta hacksaw.  I'll drop it down the hole and you shine the flash light in the hole."  Jimmy found a bone saw that was small and easy to wield.

"Ready Jimbo?"  Jack was ready to drop the bone saw inside the hole.

"Jack, I found a lamp light we can use.  My flash light is almost dead."  Jimmy looked at Jack.  Both guys were ready to drop the Saw down into the hole.

"Okay then, you Ready?"  Jack looked at Jimmy.

"Drop the Saw Jim... I'll shine the light inside the Hole while you listen for the saw to hit bottom." Jimmy did as Jack told him.

"Ah, Jack....I hear something.  it's not coming from the hole...it's inside the Lab with us." Jimmy slowly turned around to face what he had feared earlier...A Giant Snail...the SLUG.

"Jack turned to see Jimmy being slimed by the SLUG, while dragging Jimmy across the room to the other side of the Laboratory next to the open hole in the floor.

Jack dropped the Bone saw and ran to Jimmy, his gun drawn, firing two shots into the Blob like Creature.  Jack caught the creature off guard, forcing the Monster to leave Jimmy on the floor of the Lab, unattended.

"Jim...get up and run out the back door...hurry and don't look back." Jack yelled at Jimmy.  Jimmy did as he was told.

"Alright you Bastard, come and get me." Jack yelled at the Giant Snail like Creature.

Jack pointed his gun at the giant creature who was now slithering across the Lab Floor towards Jack at lightning speed.

Jack fired 4 more shots into the bulbous body of the SLUG, without stopping its approach.

Jack yelled for Jimmy to call Manny on his cell for Backup. The creature side stepped Jack and entered the hole, disappearing into the black void below.

Jimmy reluctantly returned inside the Lab and stood by the edge of the hole.  "So, the creature descended down into the hole, or is it just hiding.  Jack? Where's the Coroner and his tech's?" Jimmy moved away from the hole and stood by Jacks side.

"Dude...why is there a pile of clothing on the floor, smeared with slime, skin and bone, and a shit load of blood." Jimmy was wavering over some clothing, not noticing what he was standing in.

"Jimbo...you're looking at the Coroner and his Tech's." Jack sighed, scattering the blood-soaked clothing away from the hole in the floor.

"Wow......none of this shit is normal...We got another Alien Case Jimbo. Let's hope we find a possible clue as to what happened to the coroner and who dug this hole to Hell."

"Jack, you think?" Jack interrupted Jimmy's thoughts.

"I don't think about nothin...Jimbo...whatever happened here is disgusting and wrong."  Jack was confused about what actually did happen here at the Coroners Lab.

"Dude, The Killer SLUG is fast."  Fortunately, the Creature wasn't interested in Jack....it wanted to return inside the hole."

"We gonna take a look inside this hole or what?"  Jimmy wasn't anxious to get close to the hole in any way, shape or form.

"Let's gather up the Clothes, bones and slime.  We'll have to take these items to the other side of Pasadena, to the other Laboratory for answers as to what happened to the Coroner and his Tech's.  I'll call Manny and tell him he has a Crime scene that needs to be investigated here as well."  Jack was getting dizzy.

Jack and Jimmy gathered the remains of the dead Lab tech's Body and clothing, including the coroner's remains as well.  The Lab was now in the hands of the Precinct to investigate.

Jimmy pulled his car to the backside of the Coroners Lab.  "Time to go Jack." Jimmy sighed. "I'll put the bones and shit into one of the Black zipper bags.  Are we gonna head out to the other Lab or call it a day?"

 Jimmy choked from the smell of the slime, bones and blood that covered the supposed remains of the coroner and his crew.

"Jim...put the clothing and the rest of the remains in your black Plastic bag. Wrap it up tight with ties and stuff the bag in the trunk of your Corolla."  Jack was feeling faint.

Jack entered the Corolla, waiting for Jimmy to place the objects in the trunk of his car.

"Take us to the East Pasadena Coroners Lab. We need the pros to tell us what happened here before we go any further with this case." Jack and Jimmy were 15 minutes from the East Pasadena Laboratory.

"Ah...Jack...there's a giant hole in the middle of the road.  Something with long claws is climbing out of the hole Jack, and it looks angry, real angry?"  Jimmy sighed, slamming his car to a full stop, a few inches from the open hole in the road.

Jack and Jimmy were now face to face with an Alien looking Monster climbing out of the hole in the road.

"Ah, Jack...the thing is out of the hole, standing infront of my car. What do we do?" Jimmy winced.

"Jimbo...I'm outa bullets."  Jack told Jimmy to take a different route to the East Pasadena Coroners Lab, like PRONTO.

"Jack, this is bad, really bad. We're not gonna make it to the other Lab," Jimmy sighed.  "There's too many of them JACK.?"  Jimmy WINCED, steering his car into the curb, on the side of the road.

"Take a look in your rear-view mirror Jim....now step on the gas and get us out a here."  Jack yelled at Jimmy.

"Okay. okay." Jimmy steered his car back on the road, heading to the other Laboratory in East Pasadena.  The creatures stopped their pursuit returning back inside the hole in the road.

# CHAPTER 6


# THE HOLE TO HELL


Jack and Jimmy parked the Corolla in the Laboratory parking structure, gathering the black zipper bag from the trunk of the Car.  The immediate concern of the two Detectives was the Black Zipper Bag full of DNA deposits of the Coroner, his Tech's and hopefully the creature.

"Well Jimbo, let's take the remains we collected from the Downtown Lab, to have the South-Central Lab check the DNA of the Dead Coroner and his staff.  The creature that killed them may have left it's DNA mixed in the remains of the Dead Coroner. "

Jack told Jimmy to take the Zipper Bag to the front desk of the Sub-coroner's office, to be signed in for DNA searches.  The remains were immediately sent to Darlene, the Director/Coroner in the East Pasadena coroner's office for processing.

Darlene got a note that Jack Burton was at her reception desk, waiting in the Lobby of the Building.

"Hey Babe, I gotta a Job for you." Jack took the zipper bag from Jimmy and handed it to Darlene. "I need you to check the remains of this zipper bag for any and all DNA." Jack sighed.

Darlene's counter-part was Murdered along with his Tec's in the Downtown Lab. Jack needed answers post haste dropping the bag of bones, skin tears, blood and any other DNA that might be labeled as Alien. Jack had told Darlene not to release any information regarding the contents of the black Bag ...period. All results were to be returned to Jack Burton only. Darlene was to label the results of the remains as Classified and Top Secret.

Jack gave Darlene a hug and told her to be cautious. "Cousin..." Jack explained to The Coroner of the South-Central Sub-Lab, there's human DNA inside his Black Bag, along with one other DNA item that might be Alien. Darlene, that's the reason we have to keep these results off line. You okay with this request?" Jack looked into Darlene's deep green eyes, her forehead wrinkled when she promised to keep the remains and results secret for now.

"Jack, what have you got yourself into now?" Darlene frowned at her old friend. "A non-human DNA Jack, Top Secret?"

"Yeah, afraid so Dar." Jack explained that the non-human DNA was top Secret, Classified. "Dar, be careful...I'm not sure if the Top Secret remains in this Zip Bag are actually dead. I'm sorry, but your counterpart and his Tech's are inside this zipper bag as well. I know I'm putting you and your staff in a dangerous situation, like stepping into the Dark side of hell. "

"Okay, thanks for the caution notice...I'll do the tests myself.  Give me a couple of days to get the results.  You want me to e-mail my findings to you direct, or give the results to the Cops, or will you come into my Lab and discuss the results with me privately, direct Jack?"

"I'll Call you when the results are labeled, okay Jack? I've got my hands full right now, but I'll work through the night to get you the results." Darlene sighed, overly tired from her normal days' work in the LAB.

"Thanks Dar...be Careful...really Careful.  Your counterparts wound up dead over this case because of our involvement. " Jack and Jimmy were ready to leave the coroner's office and head back to Benny's Bar and Grill, tired, hungry and thirsty.

"Jack, hold up...You know I can't override the Political Schmucks and give you, my findings.  The POLICE will be anxious to get their hands on my report." Darlene sighed. "Really, the remains inside this black zipper bag are TOP SECRET HUH?"

"Yeah. Top Secret Dar." Jack told his cousin to be careful and use all precautions necessary to keep her and her staff alive and well.

"Geeze...our lives are in danger Jack?"  Darlene sighed.  "Maybe we should have the FBI Lab do the tests."

"No way...the Fed's will file your DNA findings in a locked Steel safe... forever. If what you find in these DNA remains are what I'm afraid of...the World is Truely facing Armageddon.  That's when my work begins and hopefully ends shortly there-after."

Jack warned Darlene to be careful again and not be a Saviour.  Darlene agreed, fearing her involvement helping Jack Burtons illegal request, which was foolish, but necessary.

"Jimmy and I gotta go now. Call me with the results.  I'll meet with you in Soho, our favorite Restuarant to discuss your findings.  Photo the results and give me the originals. I Don't want you or your Tec's to put your lives in danger." Jack was dead serious.

Jack and Jimmy returned to Benny's place to get the investigative tools necessary to enter the hole they found on their way to the Coroners Lab, earlier.

"Jack, do we really need to enter this hole?  Don't you think it's better to have the Cop's go down the hole and we watch and wait for their results?"  Jimmy coughed.

"If we do what you say Jim, all the Media Idiot's will be at that hole before we can get there. The media's cameras will follow with interviews that we can't divulge. Manny will be our only contact in this case other than Darlene.  I'll have Manny rope off the hole with caution tape and highway cones to keep all the kooky-loo's away from the hole."  Jack explained the program to Jimmy in detail for his approval.

"We can't afford a mistake.  I understand that jack.  But aren't we jumping the gun until the results of the DNA tests are in."  Jimmy looked at Jack as they were driving back to the Benny's Bar and Grill.

"Jim, Let's get our tools, guns and lights, block off the road with the local City workers help.  When we have everything in hand...the Lab Results and more, we'll make the decision to take this job or give it back to Manny.  Okay Jimmy?"  Jack looked at his friend, hoping Jimmy will relax now.

 "Who will think the hole is anything other than just a common sink hole to deal with. The city will "set the look" to passerby's, not giving any thought that something more menacing was afoot.  The city block-off the hole with tape and cones, then they left the scene for us to begin our investigation."

Jimmy and Jack made their way back to the Bar and Grill, told Benny that they will need his help regarding a new investigation that Manny Gonzales has given them to solve.  Benny was excited and all in.

"Alright Jack...I'm in."  Benny smiled, excited to be on the team again, to solve crimes as the team has always done.

The three guys packed their tools, their guns, and loaded the Corolla ready for work.  Jack made a call to Manny and told him to send a street crew to the hole in the Street.  Jack requested cones and warning tape. Manny agreed to get the City Maintenance crews to rope off the hole and keep those curious away from the opening.

Manny agreed, and got the city crews out to the hole, roping it off for safety.  Little did the Street workers know what was waiting inside the hole for them."

**CHAPTER 7**

**THE REMAINS ARE IN**

"Jack, just outa curiosity, are we planning on going down into the hole?" Jimmy sighed. "Do you think the creature is still alive? Like maybe when Darlene runs the DNA sequences inside the Black Bag, and there's no DNA found for the creature, then the game is afoot, right?' Jimmy coughed.

"Hey you two, let's hold off with the "MAYBE'S OR MAYBE NOT's. First the DNA results, right?" Benny chimed in to the conversation.

"Darlene will have the sequences ready for us tomorrow, maybe. If there's no reference to a non-human DNA discovered in the mess of Blood, guts and whatever, then we have problems, right?" Jimmy swallowed his words with a stutter.

"Tomorrow boys. No sense wasting brain cells yet." Jack was secretly concerned and didn't want to freak out Jimmy and Benny with maybes.

"So, we wait for the DNA results.  Depending on the results, we may have to enter the "hole" and face some kind of Alien Menace?" Jimmy sighed. "Right?"

"OR. "Benny entered into the conversation.  "OR, if there is ALIEN DNA, then we need a plan to stop the Alien from killing more innocents. Geeze...already over 1000 bodies were discovered, drained of them of fluids.  Let's hope there's ALIEN DNA.  If we luck out, Darlene discovers Alien DNA, then we can devise a weapon to destroy the Monster, right?" Benny looked at Jack and Jimmy with reservations.

"Look, let's hope Darlene finds DNA...Alien or whatever.  Once we know what the Alien is made of, we can kill it."  Jack, Benny and Jimmy were ready for their afternoon Whiskey Beer chasers and some freshly prepared T-Bone steaks.

"You're right Jack...we wait before we act...so let's act now for our afternoon brunch, whiskey and Beer.  Okay?"

Jack and Jimmy sighed, grabbed a cocktail table for all of us to sit at, while Benny went to the back of the Bar to grab a bottle of J.D, a case of Beer and some deep-fried chips.

"Hey You guys, you all in the mood for medium rare T-bones or what?" Benny smiled; his hands loaded down with the biggest T-Bone Steaks the team had ever seen.  "Ready for another bottle of my best Whiskey and some Beer Chips to hold you guys over, until the Steaks are cooked."

"Yeah, I'm actually hungry."  Jack sighed, tired and deep in thought.

"Then I'll fire up the grill.  Jimmy, go to the fridge and get three of the biggest T-bones you can find.  Jack, you take a seat and pour the Whiskey...okay?"  Benny was trying to calm the nerves of his two associates, without luck.

All three of the Burton Gang were deep in thought, barely thinking of the T-Bones.

"If the Alien is inside that hole in the road, someone has to go down and eliminate it...for good.  Who's that gonna be?" Benny sighed..."I don't go into holes, no matter where they are..." Everyone laughed while Benny heated up the BBQ.

"Your glasses are full.  Come and sit down at the table with me.  We need to be ready for our fate guys." Jack had poured another three glasses of Whiskey with three beer chasers on stand-by.

"Too many have been slaughtered. Someone has to kill this thing, or these things, before more dead are found in pools of Blood.  Bones, soaked in flesh, wrapped up in black, zipper bags?" Jimmy was cautious, not to blow this issue out of reason, yet.

"Drink my friends.  The smell of the T-Bones are titillating my hunger nodes." Jack watched as Benny was turning the steaks over easy, slapping his secret sauce all over the Meat.

"Guys, Tuesday's here helping me with my Patrons.  Why don't we include her in the dinner with us?"  Benny sighed. "My three servers can handle the Patrons while we Eat."  Benny threw one more T-Bone on the grill for Tuesday, grabbed another chair for her to join the Burton Gang's at Table number one.

The whole Burton team were together again, as it always seems to happen when the need is greater than the few.

The night drew on as the 4 friends filled their stomachs.  The need for more Whiskey was on the table.   Dinner had filled the immediate needs of Retired Detectives, as had the Whiskey and Beers.

"Benny boy, it is getting late, your crowd is leaving for home.  Can we lock the front doors and talk a bit?"  Jack asked his team to stay in their seats and talk about the issues at hand.

"Jack, there's way too much that's unknown here.  We're gonna risk our lives for a case that will leave us dead.  I don't like Aliens and I don't want to die today either, okay?"  Tuesday sighed.

"Listen up....1000 bodies have been strewn across the city.  Manny gave me this case on the fly.  He needs our secrecy to kill the menace and never let the world know what exists below the ground."  Jack looked at his team, staring at him.

"By the way, I fired 6 shots into the Creature at the Down town Coroners Lab.  Nothin guys...the bullets simply passed through the thing, hitting the wall.

"Jack, we're dealing with......" Hold that thought Jimmy.  We haven't agreed to take the case yet.  Manny wants the deaths to stop, and get on with our daily way of life. So do I."  Jack settled down the teams fears with more Whiskey.

"Look, we do what we do best...we eliminate the threat before it becomes exposed in real time."  Benny sighed...I'm in."

"Darlene is checking the Remains we gave her for abnormalities. She's hoping to have the DNA Results tomorrow night.  I asked her to hand me her findings and remove any link to her or her computer banks. " Jack looked at his team for feedback.

"The hard results are Top Secret.  Manny knows what we're doing and has back up if necessary...right now, we're waiting to see if the killer or killers of the 1000 bodies have DNA....possibly Alien DNA."  Jack exposed the team to a new threat that cannot continue.  The many threats need to be erased, immediately.

"Jack, we're not armed for Alien attacks.  We're a small team of e-cops that are assigned by the powers that be, to solve the murders, find the killer or killers and put them in jail or in body bags."  Benny was serious as a heart attack.

"Benny Boy, Manny gifted us with a case that may turn out to be our last hooray.  I promised Manny that we would do our best to put an end to the killings.  Simple as that."  Jimmy sighed, downing a glass full of Whiskey.

"Simple as that?"  Jimmy laughed. "So, this could be our Last HOORAY, my friends.  We are the holders of Truth and Justice, the Amerian way."

"Dude, your quoting Superman. No more Sud's, Jimbo."  Tuesday sighed.

"Actually, Wonder Woman is my Favorite Super hero."  We all laughed, half shit faced and 100% Scared to Death.

"Look you guys.  This case is more than a normal investigation.  We have remains, a dead coroner his, tech's slaughtered, and a Creature existing inside a hole in main street Pasadena on the loose.  Manny wants the killing to stop...that means we stop the killer, Dead or Alive." Jack continued.

"What does the hole in the street have to do with this case Jack.?" Tuesday asked, looking for Jimmy to agree with her?

"Jimmy and I saw some kind of a thing, leaving the coroners downtown Lab, after killing everyone inside the Laboratory.  This thing disappeared into a hole in the center of Mainstreet.  That's where we start boys.

Tuesday, you're now included in the Investigation.  The hole in the Street is holding something precious.  The creature's life and its existence." Jack frowned.  "We need to take both of those Benefits away from this Menace. Dead or Alive."

Jack was adamant that the investigation goes forward with or without the DNA results by the Sub-Coroners Lab, led by Darlene.

"So, whose going down the hole...not me Boys."  Tuesday sighed.  "I don't go down holes where something like a Creature, exists inside." Tuesday looked at Jimmy to agree with her.

"Look, tomorrow we get the DNA results.  It there is some kind of an abnormality in one of the DNA's tested, then what?"  Benny sighed.

"Darlene will bring the Results here to the Bar. She explains her results. We go from there." Jack looked at the team. "The look on your faces tells me none of you are anxious to take this case...true?"  Jack was sullen, hoping for an agreement to get the job done. "I can't do this alone."

"No, that's true. A case is what we do. However, this case is different. We got an unknown life form to deal with, like a beast or whatever it is. What we know is this beast killed all the techs and the coroner, in the Downtown Lab.  Manny believes that the Menace is the cause of over 1000 Dead." Jack sighed. "We go from there."

"Jack, without knowing what that something is, were exposed. That's our question.  We're shooting in the dark.  We don't know if the creature that you and Jimmy saw in the downtown Coroners Lab, can be caught, killed, or what."  Benny coughed, concerned about our potential success or future. A disaster available to us, pending.  The chances were not on our side. Not even a little bit.

"All you guys are right...this is new for us...we don't play with creatures that exist below the surface of the Earth.  As a matter of fact, we don't know if the creature we saw, is from Earth."  Jack took a hit from his glass, while Benny filled the other 3 glasses with Whiskey.

"What do mean?"  Tuesday asked Jack.

"We're thinking that the DNA results will show that one of the DNA's tested will be...let's say, unusual.  If Darlene gives us an Unusual, non-human Test result from the remnants we gave her, then she should be able to create an Anti-cellular antigen that will kill the creature. " Jack was getting lucid, dizzy and needed to lay done.

"So, Injecting the Creature will be near impossible.  Jimmy remembered the creature, as it was killing the Lab Tech's and the Coroner. "Look, what I saw was a transparent blob of slime, sliding across the Coroners Lab floor, disappearing into the city.  We need a deadly cure to erase the creature, permenantly." Jimmy looked at the three for feedback.

"Okay then...let's wait for tomorrow's Lab Results.  Speculation is confining.  So, we wait, we drink a bit more, eat the left overs, then go upstairs to our rooms and crash." Benny smiled, happy to end the talk about Monsters.

**CHAPTER 8**

**DARLENE DELIVER'S A DREADED REPORT**

Darlene was alone inside the Laboratory, inspecting the contents of the Black Zipper Bag that Jack and Jimmy gave her.  The contents inside the bag were inspected for DNA processing as Jack had asked her to do.

"People, time to call it a night.  Shut-down your projects.  Tomorrow we'll run DNA sequences trying to identify who the persons are who died in the Central Lab in Pasadena."

Darlene smiled, opening the door for her Tech's to leave the Lab.  The projects in process will continue throughout the night.  Hopefully, the DNA's produced from the machines will provide positive Results in the morning.

"Hey Boss, you are working late tonight?"  Darlene's assistant Coroner questioned her.

"Actually, just finishing up a project for the Police Lab. Take off. I'll be here for a few more hours waiting for DNA results.  Good night, Henry."

Darlene remembered Jack's instructions of being careful, watchful and keeping her nose outa the business of the Police.

The whole Coroners staff had left for the night, even though their computers were still running sequences of DNA found in the zipper bag that Jack had given her to process.

"The doors, windows and emergency shut off valves on the DNA machines were on timed intervals, working throughout the night. Darlene was logging in the remains of the dead Lab techs and the coroner, when she was interrupted by a knock on her door.

Remembering what Jack had told Darlene, she decided to continue her work and ignore the continued knocking on her solid metal Lab door.

After hours of processing the DNA's found in the zipper bag Jack had given her, she began matching the DNA of each of the 5 persons who mysteriously died while working in the Central Downtown Laboratory.

Darlene was logging her findings in a secret binder which she had prepared for Jack when they meet.  Jack had told Darlene that there were 3 Tech's and the one Coroner who had died from unknown circumstances. Jack had told Darlene that he thought there was a 5th person who died in the Lab as well.

Darlene was able to match 4 of the DNAs to the Central Coroner's employee files.  However, the 5th DNA found in the zipper bag could not be matched to any life form known to mankind.

Darlene picked up her cell to give Jack a call and tell him what her findings were.  She opted not to call Jack about the one DNA that could not be matched here on Earth, by anyone.

As she broke the rules of secrecy Jack had warned her not to do, she set her phone down, looked at her findings once more, then placed the call to Jack.

"Hello.  You must be Darlene, the Coroner here in Pasadena."  The locked door to the Lab had somehow been breached.  A Man, well dressed, holding a file in is hand, stood infront of Darlene with his hand out to introduce himself.

"I'm with the Central Intelligence Agency. " The Man removed a Silver Badge, his face and identify features coded in algorithms.

"Madam, I sure would like to have that note book you're writing in.  Please, hand it over to me...now."  The Agent was polite.

"How did you get past my security. And how did you get inside my Lab without entering the door code?"  Darlene scolded the intruder.

The man gave Darlene a warm smile, then held out his hand for the notebook that was prepared by Darlene, for Jack's eyes only.

"You need to leave my Laboratory now, through the front door.  My security team will escort you to the exit door of the building.  Don't come back."

"Darlene, if I may call you by your first name...I represent the American Government.  The notebook you're writing in, for your friend Jack Burton, holds top secret information inside its cover.  It would be wise to hand me the note book, then go home.  Calling your friend, Jack, will only complicate things here, between us."  The Agent wasn't smiling any longer.

"Why is my note book so important to you?"   Darlene played the conversation as much as she could without consequences to her health.

"The fifth DNA you found among the remnants inside the zipper bag, are Classified."  The intruder sighed

"Look, my findings are Top Secret.  You can play the classified bull shit on me if you wish, however, there are no findings in this book except those of the 4 persons who died in the Downtown Coroners Laboratory."

"Really, you don't have one more DNA that unfortunately is of Alien Descent.  Because of the nature of the yet to be processed Alien DNA, one of my associates will finish processing the remnants given you by Burton.

"Why don't you and I take a walk.  My CSI team discovered a hole in the middle of the Street in Soho.   You really need to see this hole in the street and give me your thoughts as to what or who created this anomaly. " The CIA Agent watched Darlene's physical actions change when confronted by the Agent.

"Shall we take a walk now...Darlene?"  The CIA asshole was tense, hoping to break her sullen composure.

"So, what are you going to do?  Kill me?"

"Oh my God, no Darlene. I would never hurt you.  It's just a short walk to the roadway where we'll find the hole."  The CIA Agent took hold of Darlene's hand as they continued walking down the street together.

"You realize it's the middle of the night."   Darlene sighed.  "You're taking me to see a hole in the street at 4am in the morning?"

"We're almost there Darlene.  One more block to walk and we're there." The Agent was respectful to a fault.

"If your gonna kill me, do it now. You surely don't need to take me to hole when you can kill me right here, right now."  Darlene began screaming for help.  The Agent tried to gag her without success.

"Hey pal, what're you doing to that lady. A jogger doing his nightly run, stopped to see if Darlene was being accosted by the CIA Agent. She was.

"Excuse me Sir...I'm with the CIA.  This lady is in our custody.  However, thank you for your concern."  The Agent was starting to panic.

"Hey Pal, you should leave now without the lady, you shithead.  Missy, you okay? the jogger asked Darlene.

"I am a CIA Agent escorting this lady to a jail cell...she was armed and now dangerous.  Please step aside and Leave us now or you'll be arrested as well."  The Agent warned the man to continue his run through the city.  "Leave now, or get arrested."

"Darlene...my name is Darlene and this man is going to kill me. Please sir, call the Police...please.  I am the County Coroner here in East Pasadena." Darlene cried for help again. "This man is going to kill me."

"Well, seems we now have an audience...so I'll be leaving now Darlene. We'll meet again, that I can guaranty you."

"Give me my note book."  Darlene stood fast, facing the CIA Agent.

"Well...we have an unruly crowd assembling around us.  Here, here is your note book. Take care and watch your back. Jack Burton will be very proud of you.  The Agent spun around, drawing his weapon shooting the good Samaritan in the face, two times.

The sounds of gun fire spooked the crowd.  Everyone began disbursing in all directions fearing the gun shots echoing throughout the area.

Darlene and the CIA Agent were again, face to face. "Sorry Darlene, all the people left us here, alone on the street."  The Agent pointed his gun at Darlene's chest, firing two bullets into her body, killing her instantly.

"I guess I lied about not killing you...sorry for that.  Sleep well Darlene. The Agent took the note book, dragged Darlene's dead body to the open hole in the street, shoving her body inside the hole.

As Darlene's body was falling inside this anomaly, a hole in the pavement had consumed the Body of Darlene, the Sub-Coroner in East Pasadena.

This Hole appeared in the early morning hours in Old Town Pasadena, yesterday.  Darlene's Body was being consumed by what lies Beneath the Asphalt of this hole. Darlene was the first to be find permanent residence in the Earthen waste land, hidden far below the ground of Soho, Pasadena.

The CIA Agent left the scene hurriedly.  Darlene's body hit the bottom of the hole with a thud, which activated the creature at the bottom of Hell.

The Dead body of Darlene was instantly being consumed by the creature below, at the bottom of the shaft below the Street.  Those living around the area listened to the crunching of her bones all night long, into the early morning hours.  Sunrise was minutes from appearing.

The chomping and tearing of Darlene's dead body was insidious.  Her body was never found.

The hole in the middle of the road remained opened...waiting...

What lies below this hole was more than broken pieces of asphalt. Getting too close to the edge of this anomaly, the hole, was food for what lies in the quiet darkness of hell.

The CIA Agent knew what was coming, but had no way to stop it.  With the note book in his hands now, he needed to seek the one person who was brazen enough to change the World and end the killings.  It was time for the Agent to Pay Jack Burton a personal call, before it was too late.

## CHAPTER 9

## DARLENES BODY IS MISSING

The Sun Rise had come as usual at 5:30 AM.  Most of the residents were still sleeping.  Only a few avid joggers were still running through the city, while the garbage trucks were gathering the trash left on the sidewalks for pick up. Noises could be heard coming from inside the hole in the Street, getting louder and louder.

As Jack and the team were beginning to awaken, Benny was downstairs doing pick up work.  Tuesday had joined Benny helping him prepare for the early-bird drinkers to show up and start their day with Alcohol twists, whatever that is.

The usual early bird drinkers were already knocking on Bennys front door.  It was time for the Alcoholic's to begin their day of joy, finding a seat at a table, grabbing a menu and calling Tuesday to their food and drink orders.

The bar was completely filled within the first hour after it opened.  The tables were fully occupied, the jute box was roaring with Elvis's songs and the bottles of booze were quickly being drained by the Drunks.

Everything was up and running.  Jack and Jimmy were awakened from their upstairs suites by Benny knocking on their doors.

"Time to Dine Gents...wake up...you guys want breakfast?"  Benny was awake, Jack and Jimmy were not.

"Come on Benny Boy...it was a late night, dude. Let us sleep for another hour...okay?  Jimmy sighed, still feeling the pings of the Whiskey from last night.

Benny returned downstairs, turned on the big screen T.V.'s then continued preparing the orders for breakfast while Tuesday served the Booze.

"Benny...take a look."  Tuesday was staring at the big screen T.V."

"The news said that the Coroner, A Darlene, whatever, had disappeared last night.  There was an all-points bulletin for locals to help spot her and bring her home."  Tuesday looked at Benny.

Jack and Jimmy took their showers, dressed and came down stairs to partake in some, Benny The Bartender Breakfast.

Jack and Jimmy sat down in the last open table, waved to Tuesday to bring them a menu and a bottle of Whiskey.  Jack looked up at the Big Screen watching the news feeds.

"Dude, you getting this?"  Jimmy sighed. "Darlene is missing, according to the news."

"Benny delivered the menu and the Whiskey to Jack and Jimmy's table. Guys, our friend Darlene went missing last night.  A jogger was found dead with two bullet holes in his face. You'll never guess what findings were found. knawed bones were covered in blood, in-circling an unusual hole that appeared out a no-where, in the middle of the street in Downtown Soho. Does any of this sound familiar?"  Benny sighed.

"Yeah, I had a meeting with Darlene yesterday to do me a favor.  Now she's missing or worse, Dead."  Jack looked at Jimmy. "So, our case just grew exponentially."

"Dude, she may have died helping us." Jimmy was saddened.  "Listen to the news. Seems some people late last night saw a man, well dressed, harassing a woman, when a jogger stopped to help the woman. Witness's say a well-dressed man grabbed the woman, then fired

two-gun shots into the jogger's face, killing him.  The Witness's said the crowd disbursed when a crazy dude started shooting at everyone and everything."

"So, the lady may have been Darlene Jimmy?"  Jack sighed.

"The news also said that some human bones, lots of human blood, were found encircling this hole that appeared outa nowhere, earlier yesterday morning.  Could this be Darlene...we need to go to the coroner's office and see if she's okay Jack."  Jimmy was adamant. "Come on Jack...we can eat and drink later."

Jack and Jimmy made their way to the East coroner's office.  Darlene's three techs were standing outside the door to the Laboratory waiting for Darlene to show up and unlock the doors to the Lab.

"Hey guys, why you all standing outside of the Lab.  Darlene's not here yet?"  Jack asked one of the Tech's.

"Not yet, we've been waiting for a couple of hours." The head Tech expressed concern for his boss.  "Darlene's never late...hope nothing happened her."

"Jack..."  Jimmy pulled Jack away from the 3 Tech's.  Maybe we need to get the remains that encircled the hole and have them tested.  The remains might be Darlene's, Jack."

"She told me she'll work through the night to get me the DNA test results of the remains from the other coroners Lab, who are now dead. We got troubles Jimmy." Jack sighed.  "Now, maybe Darlene's Dead too."

# CHAPTER 10


## A TRIP TO THE CORONERS LAB


Benny's Bar and Grill was raging with patrons.  Wall to wall people were searching for a vacant table and 4 chairs to plant their asses on. Tuesday was serving the liquid goods while Benny was dealing with the solids.

It was now 9am in the morning.  The weather was balmy.  Benny's Bar and Grill was up and running, with every table occupied. Those who came late to Benny's Birthday Party were set up in the parking lot for food, drink and conversation.  The overflow of customers dancing and talking outside in the parking lot was still growing.

"Hello....Is there a Jack Burton here?"  A stranger to Benny's Bar and Grill entered the Bar, immediately being introduced to the faithful owner of Benny's Bar and Grill, Benny himself.

"Welcome friend.  Sorry, the only tables available are set up in the parking lot. It's my birthday and everyone I love have come today to celebrate my Birth.  So, what brings a stranger like you, to come to my Bar?"  Benny was curious.  This Newby had never been to Benny's  Bar before, leaving Benny with a cold knife digging into his gut.

"Actually, I was told that Jack Burton lives here, is that right?"  The Stranger kept his eyes focused on spotting Jack possibly inside the main salon of the Restaurant.

"You came here to see Jack Burton?"  Benny took two steps backwards, away from the Stranger.

"Yes, Jack is an old Army buddy.  We served in Afghanistan in 2011.  Did I come to the right place to meet with my old friend."  The well-dressed, clean-cut, stranger, looked deep into Benny's eyes.

"What's your name friend?"  Benny carefully kept Jack out of the Conversation, on purpose.

"Jack calls me Punk..." The stranger laughed.  "You know Jack, always screwing around with anyone who wants to listen to his bullshit...right?"

The Stranger side stepped Bennys request for his name.  Something didn't smell right to Benny.  This guy was looking for more than a hello-Jack, moment.  The so-called Army buddy acted important, was well dressed and had a bulge in his left coat pocket. A 9mm pistol.

"Benny Boy...Happy BD pal." Jimmy three fingers descended from the rooms above the Bar and Grill, smelling the food.  Jimmy backed away from Benny, cautiously looking at the Stranger who was diligent questioning Benny about the location of Jack Burton and if Jack lived here, on this premises.

"Hey Benny, can I talk to you for a minute?" Jimmy felt a tug at the back of his neck.

"Cut the shit...where's Burton?"  The Stranger was adamant.  "Is Burton here, now, inside your Bar?" The Stranger removed his gun from his coat pocket, holding a CIA Badge in his hand.

"What the hell you lookin for stud.  Why do you want Jack Burton?" Jimmy stood infront of the man twisting the gun from his hand.

"Why you really here pal?"  Benny and Jimmy stood infront of the intruder pushing him to a corner of the Salon and sitting him down in a chair.

"So, you're a CIA loser?"  Now tell me and Jimmy why you want to talk to Jack Burton. Right now, you're ruining my Birthday Party.

"Say what?"  Jack had come down the stairs, quietly listening to the conversation Benny and Jimmy were pursuing with the Agent.

"You looking for Jack Burton Pal?"  Jack looked at the CIA Agent being held by Jimmy and Benny.  So, stud, you know how to use this 9mm Sally? Jack frowned at the Spook?"

"Ah, so, finally I have the pleasure of meeting the infamous Jack Burton. I have something that Darlene gave me to hand over to you." The Agent reached into his coat pocket and started to remove something, when Jack pointed his pistol at the Agents face.

"Hold on asshole. Remove your gun hand from your holster." Jack took the Agents gun away from him, while walking slowly to face the Spook.

"You have plans to shoot me...?"  Jack frowned, getting closer to the Agents face.  "This gun loaded pal?" Jack cocked the Agents pistol pointing the barrel of the gun at the CIA agent's crotch.

"Whoa...hold on Burton....Darlene game me a note book to hand over, only to you...okay...Don't shoot me for trying to do the right thing." The CIA Agent was poised to kill Burton.  That wasn't about to happen today or ever.  The Agent was searching the Bar for a quick escape.  The only way out the Bar for the killer, was in a Coroners Van.

"Don't try it bud...I feel you...you're a sleezeball...you Killed Darlene?" Jimmy and Benny held Jack at bay, taking the gun from him.  "No one dies on my Birthday."  Benny sighed.

Jack's hand was beginning to shake in anger.  Jack knew this punk was a hired killer for the CIA just by watching his demeanor.

"Where's the note book pal?"  Jack told Jimmy and Benny to shoot this putz if he tries anything fancy.

Jack gave Benny the Agents gun, then began patting the Bastard down for any hidden weapons the Agent may have hidden in his clothes.

"Burton, you're under arrest.  I'm a CIA agent and I'm here to arrest you for killing Darlene, the Coroner in East Pasadena."  The Agent changed into a defense mode, instantly.

"Hand over my gun, now."  The Agent was adamant.  "You're going to jail for murder."

"You killed Darlene. Now you're here to kill me? hand me Darlene's notebook, now."  Jack was pissed.

"The notebook belongs to the Fed's, not you.  Now give me my gun and let me put the cuffs on you.  The so-called CIA Agent tried to intimidate Jack to make a stupid mistake.

"Pal, I know what a CIA I.D. card looks like. It's not a badge like the one you presented to me.  Now's the time to spill your guts, or I swear to God, I'll kill you right now with your own gun." Jack was physically shaking with adrenalin.

"Jack, I called Manny...he's on his way over here.  I told Manny to check out this guy named Ramsey Brown, a supposed CIA Agent according to paper I discovered in his wallet.  His driver's license showed him as Ramsey Brown.  Maybe an alias? Manny ran an FBI check on the dude's name and face and sent the results to my cell.  This guy doesn't exist in any Federal Identity Banks, Jack.  He's a ghost, a hired killer."

Manny and 3 of his men arrived in minutes to Benny's Bar and Grill, looking for Jack.

"Jack...you, okay?  Happy Birthday Benny Boy....where's the CIA ghost... Jack?"

"Come with me Manny.  Have your three cops confine the guy who killed Darlene, our Coroner.  Something isn't right about this crud ball. He lied about being a CIA operative, he lied about helping Darlene with her DNA findings, then he killed her." Jack shook his head in dismay.

Manny was curious to see who this imposter really is and why he killed Darlene, hoping to kill Jack Burton as well.  Jack now had Darlene's notebook in his hands.

Darlene left a note to Jack when he opened the front page of her notebook.

"Jack, you are the only person holding a piece of evidence that could change the World.  Tell No One, Darlene."

Earlier, Darlene ran secret DNA sequence on the Tech's in our downtown Coroners Lab who were also slaughtered.

"Now, this guy kill's Darlene, takes her notebook with the DNA results of some other person, or thing.   This CIA traitor comes to Benny's Bar and Grill to kill me. But why? Just to keep the DNA Results secret? The question is...are the DNA results that Darlene found...Alien?" Jack looked at Benny and Jimmy.  "Guys, something is not right about this whole scenario."

"So, the Dick is hiding Top Secret stuff from the World.  Now he's here to kill me to keep the secret quiet." Jack coughed.  "Manny, I need the notebook that this guy took from Darlene.  There's one DNA sequence that's disturbing.   So, disturbing that Darlene warned me that the SECRET DNA REMANINS will somehow cause The End of the World as we know it." Jack looked at Manny Gonzales with confusion and trepidation. Manny, I'm gonna need your help on this case."

"Jack, I'll get Darlene's notebook from the spook.  But mark my works. You and I will be the only humans here on Earth to see Darlene's DNA results. Okay?"  Manny was dead serious.

"Yeah...we need to get the book from the Ghost..." I can't solve this case without your technology.  Manny...it cost Darlene's Life.  I'm fearing we stumbled into a dark place we may not be able to get out of."

Benny's special Birthday was a total success.  The crowds were peaceful, happy, and singing like wounded dogs in heat.  The Ghost was put in a solitary cell, with no hopes of freedom.  Jack and Manny had one giant decision to make. That decision will be forth coming after they prepare to search the hole that appeared outa no-where, yesterday.

"I'm thinking the hole on Main Street, Downtown Soho is where we'll find Darlene's Bones, resting in blood." Jack was without words.

## CHAPTER 11


## A VISIT TO HOLE IN THE STREET OF SOHO


"Manny, let's leave Benny's Birthday Party and take look at the sink hole in Soho.  The whole community of Soho are claiming that an Alien ship had crashed in their back yard, so to speak." Jack looked at Manny with indifference.

"Yeah, you're right Jack. All the residents in Soho are talking about the Arrival of Aliens." Manny sighed.  "So, tonight, you and I do a little digging inside this so-called Alien Habitation?"

"Look, It's a short walk to the Soho." Jack looked at Manny, worried that his number one Buddy was shaking in his boots.

"Jack, are you sure it's a good thing for us to enter this...hole? Something tells me we're stepping into a pile of shit that will bury us the moment we enter its house.

I was concerned about the 1001 calls to the Precinct about an Allien crash landing on Soho's main Street, Jack.. Why don't we let the City Maintenance crews do their due- diligence here?"  Manny was not anxious to drop into a hole that came from space, occupied or not.

"Let's leave my Cruiser here at Benny's Parking lot and take a short walk to the Soho to inspect this unannounced sink hole."  Manny looked at Jack for his opinion.

"Yeah, good, so you've decided to join me in the inspection of this anomaly?" Jack patted his pal on his shoulder.  Manny, there are no Aliens other than what exists in the imaginations of Story tellers.  We don't want to alarm the residents in Soho any more than we did yesterday morning.

"Jack, when my Cop's surrounded this anomaly, with their guns drawn, using a bullhorn to get 3 kids to safety that had fallen inside of this hole, that's when the stories began like a cancer." Manny frowned.

Lie after lie, story after story, people thought they saw Aliens landing here, on Earth, spreading through the city. Eye witnesses said they saw an Alien Craft heading towards the Earth, then crashing and burning into dust.

So called residents were reeling with fear, from the possible confrontation with Alien's.  The crash of this so-called Alien Shit spewed balls of fire on those close to the crash site. The Burns were like knives cutting into their arms.

"The stories about Aliens crashing in Soho Pasadena California were made of dreams that could not be heard, seen nor verified.  The surviving 3 kids weaved a story book lie, selling their lies to the News

Media, their parents and others on the street.  Fear was now prominent in Pasadena.

The catalyst that started this whole scam began with the three kids who were carried out of the hole on gurneys, screaming in fear of creatures they saw, at the bottom of the Sink Hole.

"So, Jack, The Sink hole is occupied by unknown sources...Right?" Manny coughed, whizzing, barely able to function.

"Dude, what's wrong with you? Your face is turning purple. BREATHE...settle down...it's all good."  Jack consoled his buddy.

"Manny, these three kids were stuck inside this sinkhole.  You ordered your Cops to stand down, right Manny?" No one to this date have entered the hole, to talk about it, except the three kids.

Manny was embarrassed for plotting a Police Raid at the site of an un-announced Hole that appeared on Main Street Soho.  The last thing the Cops needed was the residents and shop owners spreading the word that Aliens have attacked Soho for no good reason.

"Dude, the tabloids have picked up this sinkhole anomaly thing saying that three 10-year-old Alien boys crash landed in the Soho." Jack frowned.

"Worse yet, the parents are sueing the city for negligence, because there was no warning tape nor construction cones placed around the hole. The three kids stuck inside the hole were lucky to be alive, according to the tabloids."

"And topping off the whole scenario is the Los Angeles Times writing an article about the situation in Soho..." Jack sighed. "Aliens have arrived in the Soho, Were the headlines in the morning paper."

"Catch this Manny...supposedly the three 10-year-olds were shape shifters who came to conquer Earth. Supposedly, in another article, the three kids didn't belong to anyone living in the Soho area, or for that matter, the whole State of California."

There's no shortage of false sighting of a Space Ship crashing in the Soho, causing a hole in the middle of down town main street. But, to put this matter to bed, we need to enter the sink hole, inspect the insides of the hole for, Aliens, kids, or whatever?" Benny sighed.

"Benny Boy...we got Darlene's Note book. Within the book is Darlene's DNA of a non-human being that was detected in our Main Coroners Downtown Lab. This info is off the record and top Secret. All of this may mean that three 10-year-old boys fell into the Sink hole, are not of human descent." Jack explained the whole nine yards to Manny, under total confidence.

"Manny, I believe that Darlene's bones are at the bottom of this hole. We need to find a way into the hole, check it out, then interview the three boys who supposedly fell into the hole. I have a funny feeling that the three Boys have the same DNA as the one DNA found in the downtown Coroners Lab. Three for the price of one."

"Jack, we're almost to the hole. What now?" Manny looked at Jack. "We go in?"

"No Manny, we go down." Jack said seriously.

# CHAPTER 12

## INSIDE HELL

Night fall was minutes away from happening.  The street folks were filling the Restaurants, night clubs, movie houses, comedy clubs and more.

Soho was awake.  The street vendors were performing their tricks for patrons sitting at their sidewalk tables eating and drinking the night into absurdity.

The sounds of music inodiated the air with people dancing in the Promenade, fueling their bodies with Whiskey and Rum cocktails. Eating and drinking had awakened Soho, while Sargent Manny Gonzales and Jack Burton were lowering ladders down into the sink hole of Hell.

"Jack, the city maintenance crew will be here in a few minutes.  You sure you wanna go down inside this sink hole.  I doubt there's nothing below the street, other than a possible water main break." Manny sighed. "You still think this sink hole is indicative of an abnormal occurrence? Did you ask the city crew to provide hard hats with attached lights?  So, you think this sink hole simply happened due to a water main break, huh Jack?" Manny sighed.  "I hope you're right."

"Bro... relax, nothing is going to happen to us.  We enter the hole, take a quick look around, then return top side.  Okay Manny?"

"Okay Jack.  But if there's down there that doesn't belong down there, then what?"  Manny sighed, trying to get jack to let it drop...to let the city handle the hole from hell.

'Manny, we won't know what caused this sink hole unless we climb down the ladders and check it out. We descend below alone...just you and I Manny.  You ready?" Jack looked at his friend.

Jack was anxious to have City Maintenance anchor two Ladder's to the side walls of the Sink hole for security so Jack and Manny could safely descend to the bottom of the hole.

"Manny, you coming?" Jack was half way down his ladder, looking up at Manny who hadn't placed one foot on his ladder, as yet.

Manny took a deep breath, sighed, putting one foot on the first step of the ladder.  "Time to rock and roll my friend." Manny cried. "I don't like this Jack, not one bit."

Manny and Jack continued their descent to the bottom of the sink hole which turned out to be much deeper than their ladders were able to reach.  An additional 15 foot drop to the bottom of the hole was warranted by the two Detectives.

"Bro, turn on your minor light mounted on top of your helmet."  Jack ordered his mate.  "We gotta let go of our ladders and make the drop to the bottom."

"So how many feet do we free drop to the bottom of this hole?" Manny sighed, wanting to return top side and let the City Crews do the investigation of the hole.

The two Cop's finally dropped down an extra 15 feet beyond their ladders, to the bottom of the sinkhole.  They both splashed down in 3 feet of sewage water at the bottom of the hole, safely.

"Bro, our ladders are 30 feet long.  We just dropped another 15 feet deeper than that.  Keep your head light on and follow me."  Jack touched down on the bottom of the hole, face first into the pool of sewage water.  Manny landed just to the right of Jack, also in the sewage water, face first.

"Dude, I can't breathe in this sewage crap. Take a look to your left. There's a tunnel leading beyond this main section of the hole. Turn on your light."  Manny coughed.

"Yeah, I see it.  Let's take the tunnel and see where it takes us?"

"Dude, how did this place happen?  I mean, this isn't normal, right?" Manny sighed, feeling the coldness existing inside the tunnel.

"I have no idea Manny.  We need to continue through this tunnel and see where it takes us."  Jack continued walking through the tunnel with Manny following him a short distance behind.

"Flick on the minor light on your helmet.  It's actually getting darker inside this tunnel.  I hear something Manny...stop...don't talk or move."  Jack admonished his pal.

Manny whispered to Jack.  "I think the noise is coming from the traffic above Jack.  I don't think anything is inside this tunnel.  We should work our way back to the ladders now...okay?"  Manny let out a terrible scream, dropping to the floor of the Sinkhole, unconscious.

Jack turned as Manny fell to the floor.  "What the hell...Man.....A hell."  Jack was knocked down by something next to him.  Jack and Manny were both unconscious.  Whatever hit the two Detectives, left them both lifeless, in the sewage water.

Hours had passed since Jack and Manny were left unconscious on the floor of the Sink Hole.  Both men still had their helmets on, the lights illuminating the tunnel they were trying to investigate.  Jack was the first to awaken, confused and disorientated.

"Manny...wake up pal...Man...."  Jack was interrupted by Manny who rolled over, sat up in the sewage, looking down the long tunnel ahead of them.

"Jack, what happened?"  Manny was rubbing A knot on the back side of his head.

"Something in the dark knocked us out.  Manny, Is my head bleeding?"  Jack asked Manny to shine his light on Jack's head.

"Yeah pal, your head is bleeding...you got a big cut above your right ear Jack.  We need to return upstairs and take you to the hospital, like pronto. "Jack."

Jack and Manny returned to the surface, with the help of the city crews, caught a taxi to the Huntington Memorial Hospital.  Jack's head was cut with some kind of a claw like wound that had immediately festered, oozing a cream like compound, mixed with his blood.

"Jack, what happened to you?" The Doctor heading the Emergency Department of the Hospital frowned.  "You have an infection; unlike anything we have ever seen. I also found a torn piece of a clawlike nail embedded in your skull." Jacks Doctor was stupefied.

"Did you remove the nail from my head Doc? I'd like to see it, please." Jack looked at his doctor who was stitching up his head.

The Doctor gave the piece of "claw-nail" to Jack to inspect it.  "So, this is what you removed from my head, right Doc?"

Manny waited for the Doctor to finish stitching up Jacks head and leave the room.

"Jack, the nail removed from your scalp is from so kind of reptile.  Like an ancient Raptor like Animal.  Dude, this nail is huge.  You're lucky it didn't penetrate your skull bone."  Manny was dumbfounded.

"Yeah, but it still hurts like hell.  The Doc said there was some kind of creme like shit in the hole of my head?"  Jack sighed.

"Yeah, it's the infection from the nail.  Doc pumped you with antibody's, however, the Doc said he needed to do some tests on this creme shit from your head.  Just to make sure the antibiotic would help you. Okay?"  Manny sighed.

"Okay...so when can we leave...my head is throbbing like hell."  Jack sighed.

"We gotta wait for the test results of the creme shit.  Doc said he'll rush the tests, for us to wait until he returns with the results." Manny sighed.

"Dude, I'm fine, we should get back to this hole and continue our investigation Manny." Jack was anxious to leave the Hospital and get back inside the Sinkhole and see what cut him.

"Okay, look, Doc is on his way back to see us..." Manny was curious as well as Jack regarding the hooked nail stuck inside Jacks skull.

"Jack, how you feeling?"  Doc asked Jack.

"Good, a little sore, but okay Doc.' Jack stood up, ready to leave the Emergency room.

"Hold on big guy.my results are a bit wierd...I need to take a blood sample before you leave."  Doc took a blood sample from Jacks Arm. The Doctor told Jack to go direct to his home and recuperate.  But Doc changed his mind.

"Hold on Jack." Doc sighed.

"Your gonna stay here until I get your blood work back...understood...you have a mean infection, and this creme stuff is not normal.  So, lay down and give me an hour to get your blood work...okay Jack?"

By the time an hour had passed, The Emergency Doctor returned with a frown on his face.

"Jack....your infection is not serious...you can go home now but no work for a few days.  Just to make sure the shot of antibiotic has done its job...okay Jack?"

"A few days? Doc, we have a serious situation that needs my input, Serious and Critical Doc."  Jack frowned.

"Okay...your results were okay, so take it easy and don't overdo it...okay...rest, drink lots of water...not sewer water. Fix yourself some soup broth. This will help your condition." Doc looked at Jack seriously.

## CHAPTER 13


## RETURN TO THE SINK HOLE


"Hey guys, it's policy that the City inspect the hole, not the Cop's.  It's an ongoing investigation and you two boys need to step aside." The lead Maintenance man sighed.  "Let us do our job."

"Look, we believe there's something existing below this street sewer system that doesn't belong there. We believe there's a danger to the public." Manny explained to the lead man of the Maintenance crew." Showing the maintenance man his Police Badge.

The City Boss Man had his crew re-lower the two ladders they removed after Jack's accident entering the sink hole.

Jack and Manny's last venture to the bottom of the hole was a mini-disaster.

"Alright...do your thing."  The Lead man frowned.  The city crew was held at bay as Jack and Manny lowered themselves once again into the darkness below. Both men turned on their helmet lights and began descending into the darkness below.

 Jack and Manny had put on City Maintenance Jump Suits, water proof high top boots, and flash light helmets.  Their guns were holstered and their minds were mixed with fear of the unknown.

"Jack, it's getting colder than hell down here.  My helmet light is dimming.  You doin okay?" Manny was cautious, now at the bottom of the sink hole waiting for Jack to reach bottom.

"Yeah...I'm almost there Manny."  Jack was cautious, his head throbbing from his prior accident.

"Damn, it's fricken cold down here."  Jack sighed when he reached the floor to the sink hole.

"Benny...where are you?"  Jack turned on his helmet light and began searching for Manny.

The main area of the Sink-hole was huge and somehow growing larger by the second.  Jack was fiddling with his minor light, which had a bad connection, turning on and off at random.

"Manny....can you hear me buddy?"  Jack yelled into the attached tunnel connected to the main open area.  No response.  "Manny, I'm entering the tunnel...if you can hear me, stand down where you are and wait for me to catch up with you."

There was no response from Manny.  Jack was starting to panic which irratated the cut in his head, causing the open hole in his skull to start bleeding again.

"Manny, I'm in the tunnel...can you hear me now?"  Jack kept walking in the dimly lit tunnel, using his hands on the sidewalls of the tunnel to guide him thru the darkness

"Damit Manny, I'm in the tunnel...answer me buddy?" Jack was having a hard time breathing the further he entered, the tunnel.

"HEY YOU." Jack yelled at a giant shadow looming inside the tunnel. "Stop or I'll shoot."  Jack drew his weapon.

The shadow continued further inside the tunnel.  Jack noticed the surface of the floor dropping exponentially, dropping deeper inside the tunnel.

"Hey, STOP."  Jack yelled again.  "STOP OR I SHOOT."

The shadow stopped, then disappeared from the tunnel.  Jack was now alone, deep inside this elongated tunnel with no ending.

Manny was gone.  Jack was alone.  The air began changing from comfortable, to freezing cold.  Jack had to turn back to the original opening and call the city crew topside to drop a lift for him to exit the sink hole.

Half way up the hole, Jack heard the calls of Manny coming from below. "Guys, stop the lift.  Drop me back down to the bottom and hurry." Jack must have missed Manny while investigating the confines of the tunnel from hell.

The City Maintenance crew lowered Jack back down to the bottom of the sink hole.  Jack exited the lift, and stood quietly, hoping to hear Manny's voice again.

"Jack...." a cold voice echoed throughout the sink hole, coming from deep inside the tunnel.  "Jack...help me, hurry, the creature is coming for me." Manny's breathless whispers echoed through the tunnel reaching Jack's ears.

"I'm comin buddy...remove your gun and stand by...I'M COMIN MANNY."   Jack began walking as fast as possible in the dark of the tunnel, his hands once again feeling the side walls of the tunnel, guiding him deeper into the darkness.

"Manny, I can't hear you...talk to me so I can find where you're located."  Jack sighed.  "Manny...talk to me, I can't find you."

The tunnel took a turn for the worst, dropping into a chasm of sludge and water.  Jack could hear water splashing, coming from the tunnel, dropping deeper into the earth below.

The floor of the tunnel was wet, mostly mud and facies from above. Jack was now treading inside the city sewer system.

Manny was silent, the tunnel was getting colder while dropping deeper and deeper inside the sewer system.

Jack now stood at the bottom of the sewer system, knee deep in sewage, trying to fix his helmet light.  After fumbling with his light and turning it on once again, Jack could see the area of the sewer while looking for Manny.

"Manny, can you hear me?" Jack tried to get Manny to respond again. Still no answer.

Jack was knee deep in facies, sludge and obvious human body parts. The floor of this long tunnel was hidden in the darkness that infiltrated an anomaly that was not yet discovered by Jack Burton.  An extension of finger tunnels meandered throughout the sewer system, leading in all directions, to unknown depths further below the sewer water.

The sewage sludge was risings rapidly, now up to Jack's neck.  It was time for Jack to back track and work his way to the main room, where he started.

The area before the main salon was connected to hundreds of attached tunnels leading in every direction throughout the Sink hole.  The facies, muck and mire were engulfing Jack Burton, threatening his survival. Jack was fighting for his life to get out of the sludge and back to the Salon without success.

Sargent Manny Gonzales would have to wait for now.  Jack was on the verge of death if unable to leave the tunnels and return to the main floor of the Sink hole.  Jack cried out for Manny to help him.  Manny didn't respond to Jack's pleas.

## CHAPTER 14


## MANNY WAS FOUND


Sewage had reached the lower lip of Jack Burtons mouth, dragging his body through the tunnel to its exit point.

The end of the tunnel was in Jacks view, well lite with wall lamps, a steel grate blocking the passage of the tunnel and three small children standing at the exit point, diverting the sewage water into another adjacent tunnel.

Jack took a deep breath and let his body be pulled into a pit like area of the tunnel.  The Sewage was diverted to another hole in the sewer system, leaving Jack lying on a semi-dry floor, looking up at three children, 5 to 7 years old, staring at him.

"Hey, you guy's okay?"  Jack asked the kids.

The Children didn't respond to Jack.

"Hey guys...it's okay...do any of you know how to get outa these tunnels and back topside?" Jack frowned at the three kids who were conversing with themselves about Burton entering their confines.

"You do not belong here...you must return through the tunnel you came from and leave now, back to your world."  The largest of the three children stood infront of jack who was still laying on the floor of the sewer.

"But...." Jack was interrupted by one of the other kids.  "Leave now or we will eliminate you.  UNDERSTOOD?  A second child stood over Jacks broken body, holding a sludge hammer in his hand.

"HEY, HOLD ON. I'm not your enemy. Help me get up off this shit ridden floor...please." Jack had suffered multiple abrasions to his body as he was drawn through the sewer tunnel walls by the sewer water.

Jack sat up on the floor, rubbing his shoulders, looking at the three children standing in front of him.  Not one of the Children continued speaking to Jack.

The three kids turned and began disappearing into another tunnel, leaving Jack at the mercy of raging sewer waters heading in his direction.  The kids had staved off the water to warn Jack to leave their home, which Jack didn't do.

Jack was again alone.  The kids had some kind of power to control the flow of the feces filled sewer waters again, racing through the tunnel towards the bruised body of the Detective.

Finding himself knee deep in the first flow of Sewage water, Jack began following the three kids that entered a parallel tunnel to the one he was now standing in.

"Hey...hold up...talk to me. I mean you three no harm, hold up." Jack heard the water coming behind him.

The kids had shifted into another tunnel, taking them deeper into the sewer system.  Jack was doing his best to follow them when he had to stop, staring at what he hoped was an illusion.

"Manny...is that you.... Manny....you, okay?"  Jack saw his friend strapped to the wall of the tunnel the kids had just passed through, still breathing, barely.

"Jack, you gotta get out here."  Manny sighed.  "Just leave me and get outa here now."

"Manny, the sewer water has been diverted from this tunnel.  Let me get you down from the wall here, and we'll get outa here together buddy."  jack sighed.

"Jack, if the three things return we're done for.  They melded my body to the walls of the sewer and the walls have begun digesting my body...it's too late for me." Manny sighed, blood pouring from his back side as Jack tried to remove his friend from the wall he was strapped too.

"Let me go Jack, you need to save yourself."  Manny passed out, his body limp, hanging on the wall he was melded too.

"No way pal, we go together or not at all. Wake up bud, help me pull you free from this wall." Jack pulled on Manny's body, while the wall consumed more of Manny's flesh.

"Dude, I need fire to free you. This wall is not a wall. It's alive dude and it's eating you." Jack sighed.

Manny regained consciousness, trying to point his blood-soaked hand towards a child approaching Jack, heading direct at both men.

Jack turned around facing a child reaching out to consume he and Manny. This Child was endowed with razor sharp Tenacles, reaching out at the two Detectives who were physically broken from the collapse of the tunnel they were inside of.

Jack's arm was cut by the Childs tenacles while the Child was trying to confine Jack and Manny into incarceration.

 The walls of the tunnel were beginning to implode as the Child tried over and over again to incarcerate Jack and Manny into its make shift jail.

Jack's body was broken, yet he desperately tried to get he and Manny to safety. The Child was watching the two friends helping one another in the midst of losing their lives in the Sewer, or from "IT."

Manny and Jack were half dead, un-able to continue the fight against the Child. "You and your friend have settled for death over life?" The tenacles of the Child were moving rapidly, difficult for the Child to control. "My body is hungry. Two other Children have become ill, soon to be dead like yourselves.

"Look, let us help save your brothers.  We know of a doctor who...?" Stop...you cannot heal what doesn't exist."

"We don't understand."  Jack sighed.  "We can help your friends."

 "No."

"We are not of your world.  Your doctors cannot possibly understand our genetic existence." The Child sighed.

"Try us...one DNA is another person's Saviour...we can find a cure if that is the problem."

"How will you save your friend?  With DNA?"  The Child chided Jack with anger.

"The death of you and your friend will feed my two Brothers for a time.  After that, I must rise to the streets as you say, to find others of your kind to continue feeding my Kind.  As for you two creatures, the feeding must begin now so save my two Brothers."  The Child stood silent, disappearing into the darkness of the sewer.

"Dude, what just happened?"  Manny sighed painfully.  "The kid just left us in the sink, right?"

Jack and Manny Gonzales were imprisoned with poison secretions from the Childs Tenacles.  Trying to gather their strength and return to the street above was near impossible.

"Where did the kid go Jack?  Manny was spitting blood from his mouth as he spoke to Jack.

"He disappeared into another tunnel or chamber, I guess.  Any rate, we need to get outa here while we can Manny...can you walk?"  Jack stood over Manny, watching his friend going downhill rapidly.

"Manny, you got your cell phone with you?"  Jack was hoping for a miracle.

"It's ruined from the sewer water Jack."  Manny sighed.

"Okay...come on...let me get you up.  We need to head back to the sink hole and yell for the workers above to help us...okay...let's go."

"Jack and Manny were barely able to rise from the floor of the sewer, heading through the sewer feces and polluted water, towards the opening to the street above.

"You two will never escape this tunnel. I am right behind you and will kill you both myself."  The Kid's yelled through the tunnel echoing all the way to the opening to the street above.

The City Maintenance Crew heard the voice coming from the Sink hole. "Boys, the two Detectives are calling for us to help them. They're in trouble."  The lead man scolded his crew who were standing in a daze, not responding their Boss.

"Get the hell down the two ladders and save these two Cop's...now."  The lead Crew man ordered his maintenance team.

"Boss, why are the two Cop's yelling for help?  Something is down there, after the two Cops, Boss."  The second in command of the Street Crew told his team to stand down.

"Get your team down there or your fired...you got it?"  The team leader
doubled his fist and threatened his second in command with
termination or worse. "The two Cops are deep inside the sewer system,
and you're right. Something else is after them, so get down those two
ladders and bring them topside, safe, NOW."

## CHAPTER 15

## THE CHILD COMES FOR BLOOD

The Maintenance workers began climbing down the ladders to the
bottom of the sink hole.  The sewage water had already begun rising,
filling the multitude of tunnels to the brim.

"Alright men, we got our orders."  The lead man sent 3 of his workers
into each of the three tunnels to search and find the two Police
Detectives.

"Boss, the sewer water is rising to the lid of each of the tunnels.  We can't pass through the tunnels.  The high water has come."  The lead man sighed.

"We need to find these boys before they become Photo's on our walls.  Keep searching, sewer water or not.  Now get a move on boys."

Jack and Manny were still in limbo, their bodies broken, fighting the sewer water to keep from drowning.

"Manny, we need to keep swimming back to the opening, the sink hole."  Jack looked at Manny who was half dead, unable to swim and barely able to breathe.

"Can't do it Jack.  Save yourself buddy."  Manny coughed, swallowing the sewer water as he tried to keep his head above water.

"Bull Shit...You're MANNY GONZALES, now take my hand and let's get out here." Jack sighed.

"Boss, Jamie and Chin were sucked into a whirlpool of sludge, putrid and infested sewer water.  Boss, their gone."  The second man in command of the City Maintenance crew looked at the Boss man with disdain and anger.

"'Send two more of your crew in the other tunnels."  The Boss man sighed, agreeing with his assistant.  "Do your best...that's all we can do."

The other two maintenance crew workers were sucked into the adjoining tunnels, facing the crag-mire that killed the first three crew workers, earlier.

"Boss." the assistant to the Maintenance Leader, sent his second three man crew sucked into the darkness of the water filled tunnels, disappearing into the void's below.

"Boss, we've lost 6 men...things are not getting better."  The assistant to the Boss man, sighed.  "The torrent of water is heading towards us. We gotta get outa here...NOW. "

The city workers lost 6 men inside the tunnels of hell.  Their bodies were never recovered.  The City Boss and his Assistant returned topside to get the "Water and Power" boys to turn off the water flow so they could send more men to find and recover the bodies of those that went missing inside the sewers.

"Manny, hang on, the water is starting to drain...we're gonna be okay Manny....we're gonna be okay buddy."  Jack consoled his best friend.

"Where are we Jack?"  Manny sighed, his back broken from being tossed, dragged and smashed against the tunnel walls.  "Jack, I can't feel my legs."

"We're almost back to the sink hole and I can hear the sounds of the City Maintenance crews at the bottom of the sink hole. I think.  Come on, put your arms around my neck and I'll carry you outa this hell hole buddy."

Manny wrapped his arms around Jacks neck while strapping his body to Jack's backside.  "Ready Manny?  Hold on tight, we're almost back to the sink hole."

"Jack, I can hear voices. Jack, Jack...stop walking."  Manny sighed.

"What...huh...What's the problem Manny?"  Jack set Manny down on the tunnel floor, turning to see the Child blocking their passage through the tunnel, back to the Sink Hole.

The Child was keeping Jack and Manny from moving through the Sink Hole, to get help from the City Maintenance Crews.

The Child raised his hands, stopping Jack and Manny from leaving the Tunnel.  The Child floated quietly through the tunnel towards Jack, who was protecting his friend Manny.

"It is time to meld with my Elders....you two shall be the first to stand before the Mother of the One, who never dies. Immediately, Jack and Manny morphed deep inside their tunnel, arriving at a bottomless cavern at the end of their tunnel.

"What the hell. What just happened to us?" Manny sighed.  "Jack...my Back...it's okay now...I'm healed pal." Manny sighed with relief.

"Yeah, sure buddy, you're healed now. Dude, we're in no-where land." Jack saw the Child heading in their direction.

"Our Mother wishes to speak with you two. Please follow me."  The Child smiled, floating deeper into the abyss below the full arrangement of tunnels above.

"Where you taking us?"  Manny sighed.  "Are you the one who healed my body?"

"No, Mother healed you.  You belong to her now."  The Child smiled.

"You're taking us deeper inside this chasm.  What's at the bottom of this shaft?"  Jack was curious, too curious.

"Mother is waiting for you two...you will join Our Family and live forever."  The Child sighed with happiness.

"How old are you and what's your name pal."  Jack asked the Child.

"My name is Child....in your eyes, your world, I would be 2000 years old......now, let's continue our descent to the House of Mother.  Any other questions will be answered only by Mother."

**CHAPTER 16**

**THE HOUSE OF MOTHER**

"Jack, where we going.  The Child has tricked you...The Child is going to kill us, Jack."  Manny sighed; his body still engulfed in pain.

"We've got no choice Manny.  The tunnels are filling to the brim with feces and sludge.  We can't swim our way back to the Sink hole." Jack sighed.

"This is gonna be murder dude. We're as good as dead." The pain in Manny's body was aggravating, let alone deadly.

"The Child is ahead of us...we need to follow it or him or she to whatever its destination. The Child must know of an alternate escape route other than returning to the sink hole.  We wait for the Child to head back top side.  We follow the Child to the street above and we're home free. Okay Buddy...you hang in there." Jack was hoping his thinking was right.

"I know you followed me.  But now, you have followed me to your ending.  The House of Mother is your last day on Earth.  You two may enter the House now.  Mother is waiting for you."  The Child laughed, then returned back to the tunnels to continue securing the area.

"Well Bro, we're not topside as I hoped.  But...at least we're here, safe for now...at the House of Mother.  I'm gonna knock on the door to the house. You okay to continue Dude?  Jack asked Manny.

"Hell no, Bro. I'm in pain Jack. I don't have a lick of strength to fight if you need me, Jack."  Manny sighed.

"No choice, no options.  We knock on the door to the House of Mother and take our chances while inside, okay?"  Jack began knocking on the front door of the House of Mother.

The front door to the House of Mother began opening.  Blocking the entrance were overly dressed sentinels, armed with weapons that Jack nor Manny had ever seen.

"Announce yourselves before Mother."  One of the Sentinels warned Jack and Manny.

"I, ah, my name is Jack Burton" Jack looked around the surrounding area.  The entry of the House of Mother was open arms for the two Detectives.

"No, you must wait for Mother to allow you into the Rotunda.  Announce yourselves now."  The Sentinel scoffed in disbelief.  Jack and Manny were now considered intruders, evil, and will pay the price of existence.

The inner area of the House of Mother was huge.  High ceilings, walls of Gold and Silver, floors of garnet.  The House was shaped like a ball.  There were no windows, with only one other door at the back of the Circle.

The Rotunda inside the House of Mother was laid with chairs encircling the area.  The Rotunda consisted of 534 seats for Mother's Children to listen to unwanted travelers who were caught by the Sentinels of Mother.

"On your knees, bow your heads.  Mother is coming."  The head Sentinel ordered Jack and Manny to comply to his order.

The back door was now fully opened.  Mother had not yet shown herself.  The other Sentinel opened the front door to the Chambers of

Mother, allowing hundreds of Mother's Children to enter the Chambers and take their seat.

 Mother's Children began taking their seat around the Holy throne in the Center of the Chamber, standing.  The Sentinels would not allow the Children to sit until Mother appeared and had taken her seat to the throne, first.

The floor of the Throne began shaking.  The empty chairs were moving away from the walls due to the floor moving from the quake.

Finally, Mother appeared in all of her glory, passing through the door to the throne room, walking past each chair against the walls, inviting blessings to her inner circle of Ministers.

"The two Sentinels took their place on either side of Mother, escorting her to the Throne.  The Throne room went dark.  There were no sounds as Mother took her seat on the Throne, quietly.

The Rotunda was now lite. All of the Ministers, Mothers Children, began bowing before Mother, then taking their seat against the circular walls.

"Bring the two Convicts to me."  The Magistrate ordered the Sentinels to escort Manny and Jack to stand before Mother.

"On your knees, bow your heads in shame before Mother."  One of the Sentinels ordered Jack and Manny.

The Chamber room was filled with joy as Mother was about to proclaim the sentence of Death to the intruders of her Realm.

"Manny, did the mother take her seat on the Throne?  I feel her presence but I can't see her."  Jack was curious with great concern.

"She's invisible Jack....right?  I can hear something breathing heavily. What's going on here?"  Manny sighed.

"Mother must be transparent Manny.  Dude, take a look at the Throne. The seat is indented, right?" Jack was confused, his head still in pain.

"My Children... We have been invaded by the outer world above us.  It is your responsibility to hear the facts of this invasion against us and proclaim the invaders punishment.  Sentinels, bring forth the two Invaders and let them stand before the Throne."  Mother ordered Manny and Jack to be escorted to the Throne to be interrogated by the Minister of Law and Order.

A slovenly looking Creature slithered from one of the chairs placed against the wall of the Rotunda. It Proceeded to the Throne, bowed before Mother, then turning to face the two Humans from the Alter World above the Streets of Humanity.

"You, the one who cannot move, what is your name and your reason for invading our world?  The Magistrate asked Manny.

"My name is Manny Gonzales and I got lost in the tunnels and wound up here, accidently."  Manny looked at the Snake like Creature, hissing at his response.

"Liar...the tunnels were filled with water and feces.  It would be impossible for any normal Human to make their way through our tunnels to the Throne, the House of Mother.

"I'm not lying."  The Magistrate interrupted Manny and told one of the Sentinels to quiet Manny.

"And you, the other human.  What is your reason to enter the House of Mother?  You are a Maraduer, a killer of goodness and truth?  What is your name and why have you come to invade the Throne with your evil?"  The Magistrate looked at Jack with death in his eyes.

"My name is Jack Burton...I was simply checking  a Sink hole that appeared below our streets in Soho."  Jack looked at the Magistrate hoping the snake like creature would not approach him.

"Another LIAR.  You came through the tunnels, entering our existence far below the tunnel floors to invade our land and kill us. You are the leader of this invasion?"  The Magistrate questioned and accused Jack as a criminal.

"No...my friend and I were caught in a wave of feces, sewer water and what have you, dragging us into the abyss far below the tunnels to your world.  It was a mistake.  We had no control over what brought us to your Home. We're sorry, turely sorry."

"Again, LIAR....you cannot survive the tunnels when the water line has completely filled the tunnels...you should be dead, BOTH OF YOU...and you are not dead because you are invaders coming to the Home of Mother to destroy us, YES OR NO."

"NO. We had no plan to invade your space...this is all a mistake." Jack shook his head in dismay.

The Magistrate slithered towards Jack rapidly, raising up on its tail to face Jack.  The Magistrate was hissing as it looked into the eyes of jack Burton.

Turning from Jack, the Magistrate slithered to the foot of the Throne, raised up to the face of the Invisible Mother, whispering in her ear his findings and decision to be posed upon Jack and Manny.

"All who sit in Judgment of these two Humanoids, for entering our realm to kill US, must now vote to free them or kill them. Vote now and let your judgement stand as LAW."  The Magistrate returned to its chair and waited for the Realm to VOTE.

# CHAPTER 17

## THE FINAL VERDICT

534 seats were occupied by the children of Mother, surrounding the walls of the Rotunda. The Magistrate watched as the Children of Mother were marking their ballots, deciding if the intruders were Guilty or Innocent for their deeds, their intrusion into Mothers World.

Soon, after much thought by the Children, their voting cards were handed to two Sentinels to be counted.   Jack and Manny would receive a guilty or innocent Verdict. Justice was final in the House of Mother.

"Children of Mother, what is your Verdict?"  The Sentinels handed the completed ballots to the Magistrate for his review and approval of the Childrens Verdict. The Magistrate will then hand the verdict to Mother for her review and acceptance or not.

"Dude, who's the Magistrate talking to?"  Manny sighed, barely able to sit up, watching the voting process wrapping up.

"Bro, I don't see anyone sitting on the Throne.  Mother must not be inside the Rotunda with us." Jack sighed.  "She must be on her way here to give her Verdict to the Magistrate."

"Looks like we may have a chance of being found innocent, right?" Manny sighed, with little hope in his eyes.

"Hmm...why isn't Mother coming forward to get this ridiculous crap finished?" Jack was obstinate.

The Magistrate was still facing the empty Chair of The Throne. "Something isn't going well for us.  If we were found innocent, Mother would have released us by now?" Jack was at best, confused.

The Magistrate was talking to an empty Throne.  He was shaking his head in the affirmative, then in the negative.  But no one was seen sitting in the Seat of the Throne.

The Magistrate then handed the completed ballots to the empty chair of the Throne.  The ballots left the Magistrates hands, gliding through the air to the Throne.  But to our Suprise, the ballots were somehow being looked at by an invisible person.  Mother was nowhere to be seen in the Rotunda. So, who was sitting on the Throne, going through the ballots, while being invisible.  It was if the ballots had their own mind.

The Magistrate bowed to the empty chair, turned and walked over to Manny and Jack.

"You two invaders have been found guilty as charged.  Your fate will be the sting of Mother."

"Hold on. You know we're not guilty.  You also know that we're not Marder's or Invaders.  You never gave us a chance to defend ourselves, you just made the decision to convict us for no reason. "Now, where is Mother?"

"Mother is sitting in her Throne."  The Magistrate was remise.

"That chair is empty mister." Jack sighed.

"Mother is sitting in the Chair of the Throne.  She is looking at you two right now, as we speak, and she is telling me to put you two to death."  The Magistrate sighed, tired of listening to Jack spewing forth his ignorance.

"The chair of the Throne is empty.  Why do you keep saying that Mother is looking at us.  Mother is not in here, NOR anywhere inside the Rotunda.  So, stop the lies...you know we were caught by the sewer system over flowing...that's our crime?"  Jack yelled at the Magistrate, then began running past him, jumping up into the empty Chair of the Throne.

"See, I told you that the chair is empty...Mother is, whoa. What's happening here?  I'M FLOATING..."

"Dude, you're floating in the air." Manny was confused.  "Is Mother invisible Jack...is she holding you up, in the air?"

"Mother, shall we confine this obstipant, pathetic, creature or begin the process of terminating the two humans immediately."  The Magistrate sighed., "Mother, they say they cannot see you.  This is a ploy Mother to give these criminals time to escape.

"Bull shit. We know the seat of the Throne is empty.  you are the one who is making up stories just so you can kill two innocent humans for no reason.

"MOTHER IS NOT HERE, AND YOU ALL KNOW THAT'S TRUE...WE'RE INNOCENT." JACK Yelled at the 534 Children sitting in their chairs, not responding to his please.

"Magistrate, let the two humans see my face."  Mother ordered her second in command.

"Mother, the Humans are infected with cells that may hurt or even kill us all.  We cannot let them go back to their land."  The Magistrate sighed, calling on the Sentinels to place Jack and Manny prison.

"NO..." Mother countered her Magistrates order.

"Mother, we will become infected...we will all die from the infected ones.  Please, let us send the two Humans into the Fire of Roth."

## CHAPTER 18

## THE FIRE OF ROTH

"Jack, what the hell is the Fire of Roth?"  Manny sighed, his body turning cold.  "These Creatures are gonna throw us into a ring of fire?"

"Hold on Manny.  You wait here, I'm gonna catch up with the Magistrate.  THE FIRE OF ROTH? Geeze, what next? I will find out what these Bastards are planning to do to us.  You Rest, I'll be right back Bro."  Jack walked over to the Magistrate, trying to catch his attention.

The Magistrate was deep in a conversation with Mother.  Irrigated that Jack was interfering with he and Mother, the Magistrate ordered his two Sentinels to bind the hands of Jack and tape his mouth closed.

"Hey Pal, what's this crap about throwing us into the Fire of Roth?  We haven't done anything wrong. And Who's this Roth Guy?  You're planning on throwing my partner and I into a fire pit with a guy named ROTH?"  Jack sighed.

"Wait...before we eliminate the two criminals, let me talk to them."  Mother told the Magistrate to present the two Marauders in her private chambers, alone.

"Mother...this is not a good idea.  These two Marauders, as you call them, are dangerous and harbor disease's that will eliminate our kind. Please Mother, let me handle this matter."

The Magistrate was anxious to eliminate Jack and Manny and get back to the process of doing the business of MOTHER.

"I want you to take the two criminals to the Fire of Roth.  I will talk to them and decide their Fate.  Now...take the invaders to the Fire Pit and awaken Roth.  I want you to have Roth light the Fire.  I will be there shortly after I close the meeting with my Children....Now Go. Do as I tell you."

"Yes, my Queen."  The Magistrate left the Rotunda, heading to the Gates of Roth where the Fire Pit is located.  The Magistrate knocked on the door of the House of Roth, with three knocks.

Manny and Jack were escorted to the House of Roth.  The Magistrate stood back as the door to Roths House was opening.

"Criminals...stand back. Roth is coming." The Magistrate sighed.

Roth was not what Manny and Jack thought.  Roth was 100% consumed in Flames.

"Magistrate, why have you awakened me...I am tired."

"I'm sorry my Lord.  MOTHER is on her way here to see you." The Magistrate sighed.

"And who are these two Creatures standing at your Sentinel's sides. Are you here to send these Humanoids into my existence...I would like that, if that is why you have come to awaken me."

"Yes, but first Mother wants to talk to the two creatures who invaded our Land.  She wish's your presence at this meeting."  The Magistrate sighed.

"Ahh...I feel her Presence....Tell the two invaders to stand back.  They are too close to me and will burn before Mother arrives."  Roth warned the Magistrate to obey his order.

"Ah...Mother, welcome to my home.  I see that two creatures have breached the doors to your Realm.  You wish the two invaders to be absorbed by me?"  Roth was anxious to absorb Manny and Jack, as hunger was on his mind and in his stomach.

"No, we need to talk in private.  Magistrate, you may leave us now with your two Sentinels."  Mother ordered her protectors to leave her with Roth.

"Mother, what's happening, are you in danger?"  Roth was burning hotter as he listened to a story, a secret that Mother was keeping silent.

"Some of my top Sentinels are planning a revolt against me and my Children.  These two Humans may be of help to me, if you will hear my out?" Mother looked at her friend, Roth, for his assistance.

Manny and Jack could not hear the conversation of Mother and Roth. The Magistrate and his two Sentinels were excused, leaving the two humans free for a moment.

"Jack, this is Mother?" Manny was beside himself with the size and nature of this Creature.

"Manny, quit looking at Mother with disdain.  I'm getting the feeling that Mother needs our help."  Jack felt some relief if true.

"Roth, I need you to lie for me. I have enemies topside, among the humans, that wish me and my children Dead.  Assassins have been in the tunnels, planning an attack as I am speaking.  Our lives are in danger of elimination."

"What can I do?"  Roth was by Mothers side since the beginning of time.

"I want you to talk with the two Humans for their help.  I need to garner all the powers I can, before the Sentinels attack our Kind and Rule over the Realm.

The Sentinels are planning to kill without mercy. Me, You and all my Children.  Our existence is in danger as we speak."  Mother looked at Roth for his support.  Mother needed Roth to speak with Jack and Manny to gain their help to garner Human Police to fight by our sides.

"Mother, may we speak?"  Jack looked at the Creature on Fire standing next to Mother.

"Look, my friend and I are Detectives, Policemen.  You are in danger of a coo?" Jack told Mother and Roth.

"Your name is Jack Burton and your partner here is Manny Gonzales, right?"  Roth came too close to Jack and Manny, scorching the hair on their heads.

"Mother and I need your help."  Roth looked at the two Cops.

"Look, Mother and you are going to consume Manny and I in flames?" Jack sighed. "Why should we help you if you two are going to kill us?"

"You're right. We were going to erase you two from existence, but Mother explained to me what is lurking inside the tunnels as we speak. Mother has friends in your Police Department over the years, and you two humans can help us by returning top side and gathering an Army of Policemen to help save our kind and the Realm." Roth explained their needs, hoping that Manny and I can build an Army to fight the Sentinels and save Mother, Roth and their Children.

"What is the immediate problem Mother?" Jack asked Her.

"Some of the Humans have joined forces to attack us, take over the Realm and STEAL the SEED of LIFE that we have Protected for thousands of years.

"THE SEED OF LIFE?" What is this Seed and why is it so important to the Humans top side and your Sentinels here in the Realm?"

"All of our Children are born from the Seed of Life. Every Child that lives is because they have partaken in the ritual of the Seed and been found pure."

"Are you telling us that life only happens if a human woman is given the seed of Life and a Child is born." Manny looked at Jack.

"Children in our Realm are in danger. We are on Alert. Human Assassins have already been detected inside the tunnels, sent to kill us, take the Realm and the Seed and rule over All Life forms on your planet." Mother sighed.

"You don't have weapons to save yourselves from the Assassins and the Sentinels?" Manny asked Mother and Roth.

"We control the flow of sewage water throughout all of the tunnels that exist.  Your kind are not aware of our exact location, nor our existence.

"The Assassins have found scrolls that were sealed by your kind thousands of years ago, buried in the Stone caves of the ONE. The Scrolls were found by Archeologist's several months ago. They found a map enclosed in sack cloth, directing those living and those dead, leading to the Realm.  The ways of the SEED have sent evil to our doors. These Assassins wish us dead. They want to take the Seed of Life and destroy it.  All life in your world will end in less than 100 years, except the Chosen, who captured a parcel of the Seeds. If the Chosen gather the rest of the Seeds of life, the Chosen will eliminate the Seeds except what is needed to sustain them. All life will die within 100 years of discovery. No new children will be born without the Seed of Life." MOTHER SIGHED.

"Okay...okay...so right now you guys must have thought that Manny and I were associated with the Assassins.  I understand.  Look, we need our weapons, guns to go back into the tunnels and kill these Assassins." Manny sighed.

"Mother, there's hundreds of tunnels.  I don't know where to start looking, and, we need our weapons." Jack was at a loss.

"We have Roth...The fire of Roth....that is our weapon."  Mother sighed. "We control the sewer waters throughout the Realm as well.  Will you help us?"

**CHAPTER 19**

**THE ASSASSINS**

"Look, if the Assassins have the map, then they must know which tunnel to take to get to your Realm, right?"  Manny looked at Jack.

"The Scrolls, are there copies of the Scrolls?"  Jack looked at Roth and Mother.

"No, there was only one Scroll.  Two thousand years ago the Scrolls were interred with the Saviour of All existence.  The tomb that held the scrolls was breached by Archeologists.  The Scrolls were stolen by thieves who touched the Scrolls and were later found dead.

Those who understood how to open the Scrolls safely, realized that the End of the World and All life would be at risk.  They buried the Scrolls here, in this place far below the surface of the land above us.

Unknowingly, Sewers were built on top of our Realm, by the Humans. During the Construction of the Sewers, the land below became dislodged, contaminated by viruses.  The only parchment left was the

Parchment of the Seed.  To this day, we kept this Parchment safe."
Roth explained what had transpired, saving the Scroll of the Seed.

"How did the Assassins find out that the Scrolls were buried during the construction of the Sewer system?"  Manny was curious.

"WE don't know.  Those persons who breached the Tomb must have taken a page or pages of the Scrolls.   Our Realm is in the original location of the buried Scrolls over 2000 years ago.  What ever happened after the Archeologists found the Tomb above our Realm, is confusing to us as well.

Some of the Scrolls were found and taken, while others remained hidden. We saved what we could...The Seed of Life.  Whoever took the other parchments are the ones, the Assassins, that are coming for the SEED OF LIFE."

"So, let me see. You guys have the one document that will propagate life forever on Earth...right?  The Assassins are inside your tunnels, right now, below the sewers, heading towards your hidden Realm, to kill you and your Children, and take the "SEED OF LIFE."  Jack understood the situation with fear in his heart.

"Those of the Chosen are the ones who sent Assassins into the sewers system to find your Realm, take the Seed of Life and kill all of you.  Correct?"

"Yes, that is," Jack interrupted Mother..."We will stand by you, your Children, Roth and especially You, Mother."

"Manny and I need you two to get us top side.  We'll weapon up our teams, return to your Realm to defeat the Assassins.  We gotta believe that the Assassins are armed with Weapons of mass Destruction.  We'll have a fight on our hands like no one has ever known before." Jack already had the men he wanted to use on this mission, in his mind.

"Right now, we're light on our defense's."  Jack Looked at the Magistrate.

"Manny, you ready to make it top side?"  Jack tried to help Manny to his feet, without success. "Bro, you're gonna have to stay here and fight the Assassins if need be.  I gotta head out now to the secret tunnel and put our team together."  Jack packed a few things necessary to make his point to his followers at the Police Precinct.  Once the teams were assembled, armed, Jack filled his fighters who they were gonna fight and the reasons, why.

 The Magistrate took Jack to the location of the Secret Tunnel that leads directly to the Streets above the tunnels.

"Jack, the tunnel hasn't been used for ages.  I should go with you; however, Mother needs me here to direct her Army.  Make sure you take your minors helmet with the light on top.  You will begin your journey starting at the Earth's Crust. This secret Tunnel was dug as an escape route 2000 years ago to save Mother, her Children and the Scroll.  You 35 miles below the land mass above.  The climb will be dangerous, fraught with dangerous animals and insects.

Deadly viruses exist inside this secret tunnel as well.  You will come face to face with unknown creatures that have discovered the empty Tunnel.

There may be unknown animals that entered the Tunnels at ground level.  If so, they are indeed, Carnivores.  This will be a very dangerous trek that you may not survive Jack.  Are you up to the task to save the Realm, Mother and her Children?" The Magistrate looked deep into the mind of Jack Burton, seeking strength that will be necessary for Jack to wield, if and when needed.

"Jack, your journey through the secret tunnel will not be easy. The Tunnel was created some 2000 years ago, when the Climate of the inner-Earth was ladened with molten Lava beds and free flowing underground rivers with deadly snakes, Creatures, and killer viruses.

Roth showed Manny and I where the opening to the secret tunnel was hidden.  The Magistrate returned to the Realm to fill Mother in, letting Mother know that Jack and Roth both decide to make the Trek together. Mother was elated that Jack Burton and Roth were on their way to enter the secret tunnel and bring back an army to dissolve the Assassins attempt to steal the Scroll that held the Seed of Life.

Saving the Realm is no easy task.  The World of the past is now being introduced into the World of the Present. Jack and Roth have no idea what they're in to.  Soon, they will find themselves into the world between the Earth's Crust and the surface of the living.

"Jack, I'm ready to commence the Journey with you."  Roth was incredible, a living, breathing, Creature of Pure Fire.  One good thing, his flames will help light our pathway to the living topside and more.

Roth took Jack to the opening of the Secret Tunnel leading to the surface of the Earth above.  The trek will be difficult and near impossible for the two travelers, let alone, deadly.

**CHAPTER 20**


**THE SECRET TUNNEL**


"Roth, you know where this secret Tunnel opening is in the streets above the Earth's Crust?"  Jack questioned Roth.

"Follow me, we're close to the opening now."  Roth told Jack. "Be careful, the next few steps are booby-trapped.  One missed step and you lose your leg's, understood?"

"Okay..." Jack responded to Roth.  "We're really deep inside the Earth's Crust, aren't we?"

"Yes...But...there are life forms living inside the Earth's Crust that will be stalking us.  We're about to enter the secret tunnel that passes through the Crust.  Once we open the doorway and step inside the tunnel, you stay behind me, step for step.  Your life depends on you obeying my command." Roth sighed.  "UNDERSTOOD?"

 "Sure, so...we're here at the secret entrance to the world above the Earth's Crust, right?  We're standing at the entrance to the doorway, right? How do we get inside your secret tunnel?" Roth told Jack to shut his pie hole.

Jack continued throwing questions to Roth. "Jack, relax, I'll get us topside in one piece if you help me.  You ready?" Jack could see a smile appear on Roth's face, through the flames that consumes him.

"Yeah...sure thing Roth" Jack sighed, embarrassed.

"Jack, stand back, be quiet.  This entrance is a trap we created if someone topside found the doorway down to our World, un-wanted.  I need to open the doorway with the fire of my existence and cleanse any and all creatures waiting to consume us inside the pathway to your land above us." Roth was adamant that Jack follows his directions.

"Okay, so I'll wait for you to open the door for us to make it topside, right?"  Jack was trying to placate the "Body of Fire" standing in the open doorway pointing to a manufactured circular stairway leading upwards to the streets of Humanity.

 "Jack, follow me now, but not to close." Roth' was careful to protect Jack at all times.  Roth's body, consumed in flames, lit up the secret tunnel as he and Jack took their first step into the hidden World of MOTHER.

Jack and Roth began climbing up the fabricated stairway, prepared for any abnormalities that may face them on their trek Top Side.  Jack was lagging behind Roth, suffering from the immense heat of Roth's Body.

Jack began coughing, struggling to breathe the rancid air in the shaft. The Human Torch, Roth, watched as Jack was stumbling, missing steps, then falling to his knees.

The two travelers began their trek through the 35-mile-long Tunnel to the surface of the Earth.  The Tunnel was inodiated with insects of all sizes and shapes, along with other animals that had eaten their way through the walls of the secret tunnel.

The creatures living inside the Tunnel were infected with virus's, Hungry and angry.  these mutated life forms, monsters of the night, were watching every step the two travelers were taking, hoping for an opening to attack them.  Roth was watching Jack carefully, as the two continued their climb up the circular stair case to humanity, to the surface of Earth.

"Jack, we have breached the private space of those who now live and exist inside this secret Tunnel. That means, eyes are watching us.  Stay close to me and don't meander." Roth warned Jack. "One wrong step and you'll be dead."

The team of two made their way up the steps, with Roth in the lead, lighting the way.  A thousand creatures were affixed to the walls, the floor and the ceilings of the secret tunnel.  The Fire of Roth spewed forth his flames to light the Secret Tunnel, fend off the creatures of the night glowing in the dark.

Known and unknown Creatures were watching intently as the two travelers invaded their space.  The creatures lay in wait for the two travelers to stop, rest and partake in the morsels of food and drink that the House of Mother gave them for their journey.  The Creatures of the Tunnel were also hungry.

"Roth, it's freezing cold inside this circular tunnel." Jack was shaking. There was little space in the Tunnel to maneuver.

The two travelers slowly worked their way upwards, up the circular stair case, trying not to disturb the creatures inside the tunnel.

"Jack, the Creatures are hungry, salivating, waiting to catch us off guard." Roth warned Jack.  It was dinner time in the Secret Tunnel without a menu.

"So, Jack, what are we going to do when we reach the streets topside?" Roth tried to keep Jack occupied, forgetting the pains in his body and his mind.  The two continued their trek up the Stairs.

"We dust off the dirt and bugs from our bodies and head to the Police Precinct to gather volunteers.  We'll build our Army against the Assassins with Policemen.  Those who wish us dead will pay the price that Death Demands." Jack sighed. The Police will protect us.  They'll deal with the Assassins."

The Precinct is armed with all the weaponry needed to defeat those who Control the Assassins.  It was now time to put the Weapons to USE.

The "Seed of Life" must be protected to continue the Planets existence. Mother will be waiting for the two travelers to return successfully, to stop the Assassins and save the Planet from certain death.

" Jack, you ready for a break.  I need to find some plant life to lite a fire and warm you up.  You look like a frozen tamale. Take a load off and check the floor and walls for deadly snakes before you sit down and relax." Roth was able to control the intensity of his flames, turning down the temperature to help Jack regain his breath again.

"Jack, the Trek is going to get more difficult as we climb upwards.  Do you wish to return to the Rotunda? You don't look so well?"  Roth was afraid that a normal Human like Jack could not live through the trek, topside.

"Roth, tell me something."  Jack questioned Roth.

"What's on your mind Jack Burton?" Roth responded.

"Is Mother real...I mean, Manny and I couldn't see her or hear her.  What exactly is Mother?"  Jack was curious, maybe too curious.

"Jack Burton, you were cradled in Mother's Arms, right.  You also heard her speaking to all of us about our plan to use the secret escape tunnel to the land above, right?  So, what is your problem?  You can't physically see our Queen, MOTHER?" Jack had spurred anger with his continued questions to Roth.

The two travelers, soon to become fast friends, were inodiated with a flood of insects in the tunnel.  The Insects were scurrying for their lives.

"Roth, what's going on above us?  The insects are bombarding us without mercy.  They're afraid of something Roth."  Jack was silent, hoping the attack would end and all would return to normal.

Jack was thrown to the side of the tunnel, falling backways off of the Circular ladder, into the dark.  Roth was also hit by the Insects, doing his best to kill the beasts with fire.

After the Insects, came the Snakes.  The outcome of the two travelers was now in jeopardy.

"Jack, the Snakes are afraid.  They're not trying to Attack us.  Something Larger and more ominous is coming down the ladder, Jack.  Stay behind me and hang onto the rails of the Staircase." Roth had no idea what was about to change the lives of the two travelers.  The two friends will find out shortly what was descending down the circular stair case to confront the two Travelers.

**CHAPTER 21**


**ATTACKED**

"Geeze Roth, the whole ladder is coming apart."  Jack sighed.  "What do we do Roth?"

"Hang on with all you're might.  Whatever's descending down the ladder is too large to pass through the tunnel in one piece." Roth coughed from the smell of this unknown being heading in their direction.

"Ah...could whatever is going to crash into us, will probably kill us? Right?" Look, a giant Black Spider?" Jack sighed.  "Roth, I can see a thousand eyes dropping towards me.  The whole ladder is going to collapse if we can't stop this Giant Gorilla Spider.  Dude, it's crash time Roth....do something."

"Jack, the only trick I have to wield is my body of fire.  If this Spider collides with me, i die, but you'll live on.  Hang on buddy...see ya on the other side of hell."

"Whoa, you can't do that. You can't leave me here alone...what can we use to kill this thing." Jack sighed. "Come on Roth, light your flames and fry this thing.  Seconds to go buddy and its crash time."

Roth took a deep breath, inhaling the rancid air inside the tunnel, then bursting flames from his whole body at the incoming Gorilla Spider.

"Dude, it's working. Keep the flames frying this piece of shit." Jack was able to move out of the way of the incoming 8 legged Monster falling down the Circular Stairway to the bottom, Dead.

"Jack, slide your body between the wall of the tunnel and the Staircase. Do it now."  Roth yelled to JACK.

JACK slid his broken body off of the ladder, holding on the ladder's rails, letting the fireball of Roth and the Gorilla Spider pass by him.  Roth and the Spider fell a thousand feet to the base of the Tunnel, smashing through the door to the Rotunda that was sealed when Roth and Jack began their trek.

Roth and the Spider were in deadly combat with one another. Roth was spewing Fire to fight the creature, while the Spider was lashing out at the fireball of Roth, pouring its venom into the flames, trying to kill Roth.

Jack was way to high up the ladder inside the secret tunnel to help Roth.  Jack was now on his own.

Jack had no weapons to use if needed, except a 6-inch blade knife.  It was time for Jack to continue the Trek, upwards, alone.  The salvation of Mother and the Seed of life was now in Roth's hands, if he killed the Giant Spider...

"MOTHER, Roth just smashed through the door of the Secret Tunnel, into the Rotunda, with a Giant Gorilla Spider wrapped around his body. The Spider is killing Roth."  Manny sighed.

"Stand back Manny." Several of Mothers Sentinels attacked the Spider and freed the body of Roth, who was already dead from the multiple injections of Venom into his body.

The Spider began crawling towards the Sentinels with is mandibles dripping Venom as it approached Mothers Guardians.

The Black Arachnid leaped over the dead body of Roth, into the middle of the Rotunda.  Mothers Guardians surrounded the Monster, stabbing at its bulbous body with a deadly Virus to infect the Monster.

Jack continued his trek up the ladder.  His journey was long, fraught with disruptions, attacks and more. Total darkness was devasting to Jack who could not see one-foot infront of his face.

The Sentinels deadly virus was working.  The Spider was beginning to collapse into itself. Bodily fluids of the Gorilla Spider were left on the Rotunda floor. The Spider's body was incendiary, with a fire burning inside the Spider, exploding on the Rotunda floor.

Mother called upon her Sentinels to enter the passage way as fast as possible and help Jack make it to the street, topside.

Jack was exhausted, worn and broken.  Jack was on his way to an unwanted death.

This top Detective, Jack Burton, was having trouble working his way to the top of the Tunnel.  The Stairway climb was now occupied by an obstruction staring at him, face to face.

Four of Mother's Sentinels finally caught up with Jack.  The Sounds of the Sentinels below Jack were more than welcome.

Yet, what lay above Jack and the 4 Sentinels was waiting patiently for its due.

Within a few seconds, the Sentinels and Jack should pass the midway point of the Shaft and confront their nemesis.

Manny was close to death.  He was still inside the Rotunda where Mother had sent for her most wise and intelligent Doctors to help heal Manny.

After 4 or 5 more days of ladder climbing, Jack and the 4 Sentinels should reach the exit point of the tunnel, to the streets above.

Jack and his team of Sentinels would have to deal with the unwanted obstruction waiting for them at the top of the Ladder.  It was time to dance.

 "Jack, let my Sentinels go ahead of you. Hissing sounds are coming from the exit point of the Tunnel above us. You and I must wait here in the dark, quietly as my Sentinels eliminate the obstruction."

Jack looked at the 3 Sentinels who climbed up the ladder, disappearing into the darkness.  The lead Sentinel told Jack to remain quiet, while he too started upstairs to see what had happened to his 3 Sentinels.

A terrible scratching sound echoed throughout the Tunnel, coming from the top of the ladder. Then dead silence covered the opening of the Tunnel.  Within a few seconds, the scratching sounds continued again,  getting louder, heading directly at Jack, prepared for mortal combat.

"Jack," The lead Sentinel returned to Jack's location on the Staircase, along with his 3 Sentinels. "The threat of death against you has been removed."

If was finally safe for Jack to continue to the opening topside and make his way to the Precinct.  Jack climbed up to the final step of the ladder, finding the remnants of a Great Snake Beast, gutted by the Sentinels, Dead.  The Sentinels had eliminated the threat against Jack, helping him to take the last step back to humanity.

"Jack Burton, we're not allowed to enter the world of the Humans.  We have brought you to the end of the Tunnel.  The rest of your trip must be solo. Good luck and good bye my friend."

The four Sentinels returned down the circular staircase, returning to the Rotunda to stand against the Assassins who were in the midst of attacking Mother and her kind.

"Jack slowly opened the hatch to the Tunnels exit point, looking around the area to make sure no one could see him leaving the man-hole cover.

**CHAPTER 22**


**THE ASSASSINS ENTERED THE ROTUNDA**


 Jack lifted the cover plate of the secret tunnel, twisting his body upwards, out of the hole. Jack had felt the presence of another being inside the hole, but continued trying to exit the tunnel as fast as possible.

Nightfall had settled into the Restaurant district of the City of Pasadena, with sidewalk cafe's serving hundreds of hungry patrons.  Most of the patrons were unaware of Jack nor the creature of the night following Jack through the streets of Soho.

Jack had fully opened the cover plate of the hole, twisting his body out of the secret shaft, onto the street. Jack was now free, standing in the middle of the road, in the dark, as cars were transversing past him, almost ending his mission of survival forever.

The last 5 days of Jack climbing up the ladder to the Streets to Humanity were worrisome for Him.  Jack knew that some unknown traveler, a prevayer of Evil, was right behind him, planning to follow him to the streets above the tunnel and.......?

The likes of this Creature had never been seen before on Planet Earth. Describing the Creature was near impossible as the Monster was able to shape shift into anything it desired.

In an instant, the MONSTER shape shifted into the bodily form of Jack Burton, as it exited the secret tunnel.

The creature escaped the secret tunnel following Jack to the Precinct. The Game was now afoot as the saying goes.

Jack was on his way to the Police Precinct to gather a team to follow him back down the Secret Tunnel, to the Rotunda, and fight the Mutant Assassins.

This Middle Earth Monster following Jack was spewing a liquid from its mouth, meant to kill any living Human who dared to attack it.

The existence of Humanity was in peril, with Jack running from this Bulbous, transparent goal, making his way to the Police Precinct.  Jack entered the Police Building with the creature right behind him.  Within seconds the Officers inside the Precinct were consumed.  Jack stood alone staring at the creature, licking its mouth, looking for more meat to eat... then looking at Jack.

 The Monster had entered the Police Station, ravaging every Human being except Jack Burton.

The creature had spotted Jack hiding among the furniture, computers and more.  Jack Burton was the only human left in the Police Building, alive.

The Creature from the Sink hole looked at Jack, snarling, drool dripping from its mouth.  The liquid burned its way through the floor of the Police Building to the lower level of the structure. Jack saw his chance to make it down to the basement of the building while the creature was occupied finishing its dinner.

The creature searched the entry floor of the Police Building, now covered in fleshless bones, looking for Jack Burton.  Jack was hiding in the darkness of the basement below, hoping that the Monster would give up looking for him and leave the premises.  That did not happen. Soon, the two would come face to face for the final battle.  The loser would pay the price of the Grave. The Victor would continue its trek to greatness.

The Rotunda was buzzing with Sentinels preparing for battle.  Manny was cared for, healed by the hands of the Matron.

Mother had gathered her clan in the Rotunda, warning her kind that her Sentinels who escorted Jack through the tunnel, fell prey to a creature  inside the Secret Tunnel.

The Golden and Silver doors leading to the Rotunda, smashed open, startling all who were gathered to fight the Assassins.  Mother's House was breached. The battle had begun.

## CHAPTER 23

### JACK RETURNS TO THE ROTUNDA

Jack made his way out of the basement of the Police Station, back to the secret hole.  The Police were literally consumed by the Monster in seconds.

Jack watched his friends eaten by the creature, spitting out their bones on the floor of the Precinct. There was no time to waste.  The battle in the underworld had begun.

The hole to the secret tunnel had been breached by someone or something.  It was difficult for Jack to enter the tunnel without falling thousands of feet below, to his death.

Turning to a street crew who were in the process of cleaning up the debris, Jack asked the team leader if there was another access point to the sewer tunnels below ground.

"Look bud, you're not allowed to enter the sewers.  first its too dangerous.  Second, it's too dangerous.

"I have a friend who accidently fell into the sink hole.  Can you lower me down the hole and help me save my friend from a certain death?" Jack sighed, hoping the Leader of the Maintenance crew would help him.

"Like i said pal, no one goes into the Sewer system without my knowledge.  Least of which, a local like yourself." The crew leader frowned at Jack and denied his request.

"My friend fell down into to the sewers.  You gotta help me save his life...please." Jack pleaded with the Crew Chief.

"okay, you stay put." The Crew Chief ordered his men to open the manhole and go into the sewers and find the friend of Jack who fell into the mess below.

A large machine was brought to the site, stationed over the secret hole to Mothers House.  5 maintenance crew were lowered into the hole by the machine.  The 5 men turned on their helmet lights and were lowered to the sewer, some 50 feet below the surface.

Jack watched as the street crew were lowered into the darkness below the surface of the hole.  A beam of light burst from below, illuminating the insides of the hole.  The 5 Crewmen were incinerated.

The Leadman of the maintenance Crew told the machine crew to bring the lines back up to the street level, pronto.  All 5 bodies were returned topside, boneless, flesh only.

"What the hell is down inside this hole?"  The leadman grabbed Jacks shirt, dragging him to the edge of the open hole.

"What's going on here?  You killed my men you prick.  What's down inside this sewer?"  The lead man was standing next to the open hole holding on to Jacks shirt, when a transparent blob grabbed the Street worker and consumed his body.

Jack stood to the side of the hole, lowering his body down into the sewer while the Crew Chief was engulfed by the creature.  The staircase was still in effect.

Jack began descending down the staircase, heading down into the darkness to the alter world.  Time was a factor, leaving Jack with no options to get to the Rotunda to warn Mother of the existence of the creature killing all who came in contact with the Blob.

MOTHER had sent 3 more Sentinels up the ladder to the street surface to retrieve Jack and return him to the Rotunda below.  Meanwhile, the battle between the Assassins and the Sentinels was well underway.

It would take Jack at least 10 to 15 days to reach the Rotunda, Mothers house.  With the Assassins already engaged with the Sentinels, the battle was growing exponently.  Jack was afraid he wouldn't reach the Rotunda in time to help save the SEED OF LIFE.  The fight against the Assassins was a losing battle for MOTHER.

By the time Jack made his way to Mothers House, the Rotunda was laced with dead bodies of the Sentinels and Assassins strewn throughout Alter land.  Jack stood in dismay as he searched for Manny and for MOTHER.

"Bro, Manny, you okay?" Jack found his friend among the pile of the dead.  Mother was nowhere to be found.  The Rotunda was in shambles, barely standing upright.

Jack helped his friend up and both men began searching the Alter World for Mother, the Sentinels and the Assassins.

"Dude, there's more Assassins heading towards the Rotunda."  Manny sighed.  "The Assassins are looking for the "SEED OF LIFE."

"Manny, do you know where the Seed of Life is?"  Jack asked his friend.

"I got it Jack.  I took it away from Mother after the Alien Assassins killed everyone here, inside this Alter World, including MOTHER.  The bastards will be returning soon.  We need to get out a here."

"Where's the SEED OF LIFE, MANNY?"  Manny removed a golden box, inserted the key to open the box, showing Jack the insides.  The seed of life was safe for now.  Manny was right, it was time to go back top side.

"Bro, we've got killers descending through the secret hole, plus Assassins coming at us from another location existing in this Alter World.

The Shaft is dead to us.  We need to find our way back to the streets above this World, by taking the Assassins route...that's our only hope for us to survive and save the Seed of Life."  Manny was right, but a little late on the game plan.

"Bro, I hear the footsteps of the Assassins entering our Space.  The Rotunda is gone.  We need to hide, make our move when the time is right and get back topside."  Jack sighed. "You able to fight if needed?"

"Oh yeah, I'm ready to fight these bastards." Jack, there's a cave like space that the Assassins aren't aware of. We can hide there until it's safe.

The Assassins will be making their way through the front door of the Rotunda in seconds.  Jack and Manny will stay in hiding, with the Seed of Life in their possession, waiting til the Assassins are destroyed inside the Rotunda by the Sentinels.

The Assassins found a hidden access point, cutting through the Mountains, going down below the Crust of the Earth.  The Sentinels who guard the top of the World, watched as the Assassins were making their way to the opening.

The Sentinels sent warnings down through the Earth's Crust, to the House of Mother.  The Top of the World had been breached by the Assassins.

The main Army of the Sentinels were in waiting inside the Rotunda, prepared for battle.   The Assassins would soon, break through the blockades of Mother, to their death.

"Lead the way buddy."  Jack held the Box that holds the Seed of Life, in his shaky hands.  The two Detectives made their way to the hiding place that Manny had found earlier, just outside of the Rotunda door.

"Jack, if and when the Assassins break through the 12-foot-thick walls of the Rotunda, the Sentinels will eliminate them.  We need to take the access road back up to the surface and stop the advance of the Assassins."  Manny sighed.

"Manny, if we don't get the Seed of Life to the Humans top side, the World will die.  No matter what happens, you and I need to propagate the World with the seeds.  The rebirth of humanity and all life forms will restart.  All of what is left of Humanity will begin again with the Seeds implanted inside of them." Jack waited inside the hiding place outside of the walls of the Rotunda.

"Jack, I can hear footsteps coming through the Earth's Crust.  I think it's the Assassins.  This will be their final battle if they can't find the Seed of Life.  They too, will all die if they can't retrieve the Seed of Life.  Shhh...their coming Jack.  Shhh." Manny took a deep breath, as the Assassins passed by his secret hiding place.

"Jack, the Assassins will breach the doors of the Rotunda in a matter of seconds.  Mother and her Sentinels will all be slaughtered."  Manny sighed.

"Manny, we can't help them now...we need to return to the streets above this place, plant the seeds of life before the Assassins return you with me?"  Jack looked at Manny's face, broken and scared.

**CHAPTER 24**

**HIDING FROM THE ASSASSINS**

"Manny, the Assassins will surely see us and take the Seed of Life.  We need to go deeper inside this hiding place and stay out of sight.  Follow me Manny."  Jack was interrupted by Manny.

"Jack, MOTHER can be invisible.  We need to get her, hide her with us inside this hole, until the Assassins are destroyed."  Manny sighed, hoping that Jack would understand.

"You want us to return inside the Rotunda, grab Mother and take her with us to the hole in the Earth's Crust?"  Jack sighed.  "You gotta be kidding."

"Without Mother, the Seed of Life cannot be born.  The Seed has to be ingested inside of MOTHERS body to germinate.  You understand Jack?"  Manny sighed.

"Shit...so how do we get back inside the Rotunda, explain to Mother what we're doing and why, then make our way to the hiding place you found?"  Jack shook his head in dismay.

"Without Mother, Planet Earth is going to die, like tomorrow."  Manny sighed.  "We need to get back inside the Rotunda, get Mother and return to our hiding place.  The sounds of the Assassins trudging through the Earth's Crust is non-stop, there's no time to talk."  Manny was angry.

"OKAY...okay...let's go...sounds like the Assassins are still running through the Earth's Crust as we speak.... "Question?"  Won't the Sentinels inside the Rotunda keep us from taking Mother to the Surface topside?"  Jack sighed.

"Remember, Mother is Invisible.  We get inside the Rotunda, past the Assassins, without the Assassins knowing we breached the doors to the Rotunda.

We find Mother who I believe is waiting for us. Okay?" Manny coughed, hopeful. "Jack, we need to return to the Rotunda, get Mother and make our way back to the Earth's Crust, then take the road to the street, top side."

The two Detectives ran back to the Rotunda wall, finding the entry doors smashed open.  Manny yelled to the Sentinels that we needed to protect Mother and take her topside to propagate Life that may still exist after this Holicost."

The gates to the Rotunda were hanging on their hinges, broken.  The Army of the Assassins were in attack mode, killing everything inside the Rotunda walls. Mother had to be found or all is lost.

"Jack, we gotta hurry, get inside, find Mother and leave the Rotunda before the Assassins see us and incarcerate us."  Manny was shaking.... nervous.

"Manny, the Assassins are already inside the Rotunda....we go inside the gates and the Assassins will kill us, the Sentinels and probably Mother as well.  The game is over Manny." Jack sighed.

"We gotta go inside Jack...without MOTHER, the World cannot be re-populated.  Come on, run Jack, like your life depends on it."  Manny yelled at Jack who was staring at the Army of the Assassins entering the Gates of the Rotunda, non-stop.

"Shssss...Something or someone is coming to the Rotunda.  Hold on...I think it's more Assassins looking for us and Mother."   Jack looked at Manny.  "I can't see her, but I think Mother is with us now."

"Yes....I am with you. We need to rise to the streets above, where humanity is being attacked by the Army of the Assassins."   MOTHER whispered to Jack and Manny who were still hiding in their cave like space, confused, ready to run inside the Rotunda and save Mother.

"Jack...Manny...I am with you two now. We need to leave this place before the Assassins get here.  Their already in the Alter World looking for us."  MOTHER sighed.  "You two boys still have the Seeds of Life?"

"Yes Mother, I'm holding onto the Seeds.  I can't see you...can you become transparent?" Jack looked at Manny, looking for his help.

"Jack Burton, if you see my real existence, you will die.  Trust me...open your minds and connect with my mind.  We must go topside now. There is a WAR here in the Earth's Crust and another WAR top side, destroying my Creations, your Humanity.  We must hurry to save the last few who are needed to re-populated the Planet, Understood boys?"

"Mother, there's Assassins all over this place.  It's gonna be near impossible to escape the eyes of the Assassins who will see us." Jack sighed.

"I told you boys to connect to my mind.  Think of me and you two will become invisible, like me.  Trust me boys."  MOTHER sighed.

# CHAPTER 25

## INVISIBLE-HIDDEN

Jack and Manny were stupefied, confused,  not understanding that an Invisible Creature called Mother was calling their names to stand beside her.

"Dude, are you hearing the voice of Mother?"  Jack asked his friend.

"Yeah, I hear her, I think.  Is she here with us now?"

"Boy's, you need to believe in me...I am here.  We need to take the main tunnel up to the streets of the Humans, NOW."

"MOTHER....where are you?"  Jack asked the voice calling him to come to her side.

"I am everywhere Jack Burton...there is no time for you and Manny to play games.  Follow me to the tunnel the Assassins.  The Assassins use this tunnel to descend to the Rotunda.  They're also occupying the tunnel leading topside, to the streets of the Human's.  Now...these Dog like Wolves are in a position to destroy My Rotunda."  MOTHER SIGHED.

"OKAY..." Jack sighed, relunctant to obey an unseen voice that could take them to their end. A Dead End.

"Manny, do you have the Seed of Life with you?"  Mother asked him.

"Ah, yeah?"  Manny was worried that Mother could read his mind. Manny heard a voice from an invisible being.  The Voice was not that of MOTHER.  Someone else had entered Manny's mind.

"Dude....you believe MOTHER is here with us now.  What if the Real Mother isn't here with us now, and it's one of the Assassins reading my mind?  What if We're suffering a brain freeze Jack.  This voice wants us to give it the Seed of Life...what if it's not Mother inside my mind?"

"Boy's, we need to take the Assassin's tunnel to the surface above, to seed what is left of the Population.  Armageddon has wiped out every living creature existing on the surface of the Planet."  Mother sighed, prodding the two men to follow her to the surface of the Planet.   Time was not in their favor.

"It's gonna be a long walk Mother, in the dark, in the Assassin's Tunnel....how long before we get to the top of the World?"  Manny sighed, not believing that Mother was really with them...Jack and Manny felt that their minds that had been tricked by some other power, wanting the Seed of Life.

"Take my arms and hold on tight."  Mother warned Jack and Manny.

"What, hold on to your arms? I can't even see you.  How do I hold onto your arms if I can't see you?"  Manny coughed up sputum, irritated with Mothers orders.

"Manny, reach out to her voice and take hold of whatever your hands feel.  We need to get top side.  More Assassin warriors are descending down through this tunnel.  Dude, we need to hold on to Mother and go Invisible....NOW."  Jack pushed Manny forward to reach out for Mother, before the Assassins could see them and kill them.

Jack's plan worked.  Manny and Jack reached out for the invisible body of Mother, turning them invisible.  The Assassins arrived at the site of the three, sniffing like dogs for the smell of the three hidden in the dark, invisible with Mother.

After a few minutes of being sensed by the Assassins, the Assassin Leaders ordered their warriors to continue to the Rotunda and finish the fight, to seize the "SEED OF LIFE, and kill MOTHER.

The Sentinels had lost 90 % of their warriors to the Assassins.  The battle was almost over for the Underworld.

MOTHER, Jack and Manny continued their trek up through the tunnel to the surface of Earth.  When they finally arrived top side, the horror of War had left the dead laying on the ground, inside buildings, homes, Churches and more.  The World was hurt and bleeding.

Death had covered the Planet.  Jack and Manny were stepping over bodies that were slaughtered, searching for anyone still alive.

"Boy's, continue searching for survivors.  The Seeds need to be implanted in the dead as well as the living.  The Assassins will be here soon.  Time is not on our side."  MOTHER SIGHED.

"So, what do we do?"  Manny sighed.  "Mother, we have no weapons."

"We have the Seeds of Life that will revive the Dead and feed the living. If we hurry, we can save the World and those existing throughout the Surface of the Planet, by being seeded.  Hurry, continue seeding the dead while I search for the Living."

Mother began her search, leaving large amounts of the seeds with Manny and Jack to feed the dead.  MOTHER's job is to find the living and revive their souls to defeat death.

"Bro, give me half of the Seeds and you keep the other half.  Mother said we simply open their bodies, even if dead, torn and broken, implant one seed in each of the bodies we find."  Jack shook his head in dismay.  "At this rate, we'll be dropping seeds til the World comes to an end."

"What do you mean Jack.  We gotta revive Humanity and all other life forms as well."  Manny was in the process of seeding the World to those who were still breathing and those who were not.

"There has to be a faster way of seeding the Earth.  And don't forget, the Assassins will finish the War below and return top side to finish us....

When they find out that the Seeds of Life no longer exist in the Alter World, they'll be back here in a flash.  We need to spread the seeds into the air...that's the only way to seed the Planet before the Assassins return topside."  Jack looked at Manny.

Mother continued her search alone, for anyone alive.  The boys took handfuls of the seeds and began spewing them into the air.  The system they chose was awakening the dead, slowly.

The boys needed some kind of a huge, giant fan to spread the seeds faster.  That kind of a Fan did not exist, but the whirlwinds ravaging the burned and torn lands throughout the Planet did.  The seeds were being strewn rapidly, awakening Humanity.  Luckily, there were no signs of the Assassins as yet.

**CHAPTER 26**

**ASSASSINS RETURN TOPSIDE**

"Okay Manny, we're spreading the seeds faster than we can count those DEAD."  Jack was throwing the seeds into the winds.  The Revival of the lost was at hand.

"Jack, where's Mother?" Manny sighed.  "I'm running out seed."

"Keep seeding Manny.  Mother is doing her thing, I think.  Anyhow, keep seeding the Dead and I'll seed the lost."  Jack and Manny were all out to do what was needed to return Earth and Humanity to normality.

"Jack, do you hear what I hear?"  Manny sighed, stopping his seeding to face their nemeses, the Assassins.

"Shit...their back...now what do we do Jack."  Manny sighed, watching the Assassin's exiting their tunnel, heading post haste towards Manny and Jack.

"Stop, drop the Seeds to the ground, put your hands behind your backs." One of the largest Assassins held a katana sword against the neck of Manny.

"Jack.... J.a.c.k.  What do we do now."  Manny sighed, still holding a basket of seeds yet to be germinated.

"Turn around Manny...the seeds are working...the dead are rising to stand with us." Jack yelled at Manny. "Keep throwing the Seeds."

"I told you two to STOP. Do not throw the seeds. You must stop now, or suffer the Hounds of Hell." The largest of the Assassins raised his hand with his sword like spear in hand.

The night had settled onto the lands throughout the Planet. The Dead were being resurrected as were the living who had been attacked by the Assassins earlier.

The Humans were awakening from the grave, watching the Assassins attacking Manny and Jack. Mother was nowhere in sight.

"Jack, more Assassins are exiting the tunnels from the Alter World. They're gonna kill us, Jack."

"NO, THEY'RE NOT....YOU AND JACK CONTINUE SEEDING THE EARTH, I WILL DEAL WITH THE ASSASSINS." Mother sighed, looking at the entourage of Assassins exiting the Tunnel from the Alter World. Invisibility was the only weapon the two travelers had to wield.

The winds of time were awakening as were the dead. Time was not on the side of Mother and her two Sentinels, Jack and Manny.

The Assassins were killing the risen faster than the three Guardians could speak. "Boys, come to me. NOW." Mother held out here hands to embrace Jack and Manny.

"Dude?" Manny sighed.

"Do as she ask's Manny.  Reach out."  Jack had already raised his arms to embrace Mother, disappearing into the winds of time.  Manny followed, relunctely, embracing Mother, disappearing as well.

"Jack, we're inside of a bubble...I can see the Assassins looking pissed off that we disappeared.  Their starting to remove their katana swords, cutting the air in every direction to spot us and kill us."

Manny was thrilled the moment he touched the arms of Mother.  His life excelled exponently with a power he couldn't control.

Jack too, after embracing Mother had the same feelings, blowing his mind, in a good way.

"Boys, you need to continue sowing the seeds.  You'll continue being invisible until I return."  Mother instructed the two newly appointed Guardians to do her bidding.

Mother disappeared into the heavens, sewing her bundle of seeds apron the land below.  Mother was moving as the light of the Earth was being rekindled.  People we waking up from death, confused, not seeing Mother, only hearing the sound of her soft voice filling their souls with love.

"Dude, I'm running out of Seeds."  Manny smiled at Jack.  "We're doing something good, right."

"Amen, bro....something good.  The Assassins have stopped.  They're just standing in the location where we disappeared, looking around the area for something, maybe us, I think.  "Right?" Jack had a few bundles of seeds he shared with Manny, continuing their work, as Mother Directed them to continue seeding.

The Leader of the Assassins directed his killers to make a Hugh circle from inside the Rotunda.  The circle inside the Rotunda involved an area over 1000 square feet.  The Killers did as they were instructed.

"ASSASSINS, REMOVE YOUR SWORDS. START WALKING TOWARDS THE CENTER OF THE CIRCLE, BRANDISHING THE KATANA'S.  WE HAVE THE TWO MALES AND MOTHER CAPTURED INSIDE THE CIRCLE....WALK SLOWLY....BRANDISH YOUR KATANA'S.  KILL THE INVISIBLE BASTARDS AND SPIT ON THEIR GRAVES." The Leader of the Assassins ordered his men.

The circle was set and the Assassins began walking towards the center of the circle to capture the three of us.  Whatever was inside the circle, will suffer death at the blades of the katana.

"MOTHER....we're all inside this circle. Now what?"  Jack looked at MOTHER.

"Jack, I'll call upon the maker of Lightning.  We are at risk, so stay in the center of the Circle until I make contact with the Maker."  Mother left the two inside the Circle made by the Assassins.

The Circle was now in place.  The order was given for the Assassins to close in on the Circle, brandishing their katana swords, slicing the air infront of them.

"Dude, while we're waiting for Mother to return, the circle will close in on us.  Bro, we're doomed."  Manny sighed.

"We gotta hope that Mother can get back here and stop the circle from closing."  Jack was worried that their fate was at hand.

"You think we could snatch a katana from two of the 1000 Assassins circle and fight back?"  Manny sighed, lost for options.

"Manny, 1000 Assassins against the two of us. We need to wait for MOTHER to return.  She said she was gonna meet with the Maker, right?  So, what does the Maker, make?"  Jack sighed.

"I don't know Jack, maybe lightning bolts or something."  Manny was again out of options.

"Bro, the Assassins are closing in on us, like fast...we need MOTHER to get here like now, or kiss our lives goodbye dude." Jack and Manny were on hold.  No more options were available, except one, Death.

**CHAPTER 27**

## THE CIRCLE OF DEATH

"Dude, what's that sound...sounds like a train is coming from below the surface of the streets."  Manny sighed.  "Is it Mother?"

"Manny, did you see the Assassins, in the flesh?  You know what they look like, SOUND LIKE....right?"  Jack felt the ground under his feet vibrating as well.

"It's time to go...We can continue the seeding when we find Mother." Manny looked at the asphalt road under his feet beginning to crack open.

One Assassin's head appeared after another from below the streets. Hundreds of Animal-like killers had breached the opening and raced towards Manny and Jack.

"Manny, RUN...NOW..." Jack yelled at Manny as hundreds of dog-like Assassins came ripping the street apart, racing directly at Manny and Jack.

"Where the hell is MOTHER Jack."  Manny cried, running beside Jack as they tried to get away from the Animals.

"Jack, Manny....listen to the wind. You two have the ability to fly...do it now."  MOTHER's voice echoed across the skies, while she was riding on Lightning bolts in the Heavens.

"What the hell."  Jack was stupefied. "Mother, come and get us.  The Assassins Dogs are on our tails."

"Grab the wind...the wind will save you until I can get to you both." Mother's voice echoed throughout the land, scaring the Assassin Dogs.

The Dog's stopped, listened to the voice of Mother smashing into their brains from the heavens above. The cries of pain the Devil Dogs were subjected too, caused them to stop their attack on Manny and Jack, temporarily.

Hundreds of Animals were staring at the skies above them, watching lightning bolts snapping about their bodies.  It was time for Jack and Manny to grab the winds and rise above the streets to Mothers side.

"Have you two boys finished seeding the dead?"  Mother gathered Jack and Manny to her side, protecting the two Detectives from the wolf like dogs.

"We're flying. We're really high up, in the midst of this lightning storm." Jack sighed. "MOTHER?  Where are we going?"

"Jack Burton, we are going to the top of the World, the Mountain of Life.  There, you and Manny will oversee the risen below, on Earth."

Renewed life must be protected.  I will give you my powers over the sky's.  Use the lightning bolts to stop the Assassin Wolves.  They're many and can only be killed with my lightning shards."

"Where are you going?"  Manny asked the God like Creature called Mother.

"My work is finished here. You and Jack will continue spreading the seeds you have left, eliminate the Assassin Wolves, then resume your normal lives thereafter."  Mother smiled lovingly at her two Human Guardians. "You two have done well."

"Will we see you again Mother?"  Manny and Jack were captured in the whirlwinds of time and sent to the top of the highest Mountain, to oversee the elimination of the Assassin Wolves below, on the surface of the Earth.

"Ah....Jack...we just landed on top of the highest Mountain on Earth." Manny looked confused.  "Yet, I can see everything below, on the ground, around the Earth, clearly...how is this possible."

"We're Guardians Buddy....Mother has given us some magic or something, to finish her work, save the lost and eliminate the Assassin Dogs forever."  Jack sighed.

"How Jack...how do we sit on top of this mountain and dictate to the Living below that everything will be okay, someday."  Manny looked over the edge of the Mountain top magically able to see the ground below, clearly.

"We don't dictate...we help the New Age that Mother just created to continue growing.  Life shall resume as before." Jack smiled at Manny.

"The Devil Wolves need to be eliminated first, right?" Manny looked at Jack.  "Are we some kind of God's now?"

"I don't know. But there's one thing I do know.  We're here because of Fate Manny.  No other reason." Jack and Manny continued overlooking the surface of the land below, making sure all was as predicted by MOTHER.

"The Dogs are evaporating Dude...are you seeing what's happening below?"  Manny was confused.  "Why are the Wolves disappearing Jack?"

  "Hell, I have no idea..."Jack sighed. "

"Yeah, is it because we're Guardians NOW? right? but Mother is gone...for good?"  Manny questioned Jack.

"No, She's still somewhere in the voids.  We need to continue the fight against the Assassins and end the War.  That's what Guardians do."

"Look. I think we're supposed to eliminate the Wolves, revive the dead, restore whatever. Shit...I have no idea what's happening to us. We need to find Mother and have her explain what we're supposed to do, okay?"

"We're Guardians Jack...So that's what we are...?"  Manny sighed.

"We're floating pretty high up in the sky.  You ready to finish the job Manny?"  Jack started to descend to the surface of the Earth.  "Come on, follow me."

"Wait up. Mother thinks we have to restore the World back to its beginning."

Destroy the Assassins and save the Seeds, right?" Manny looked at Jack.

"Yeah...A new Beginning buddy...we're in the midst of creating a new Beginning.  We need to eliminate the Wolves...right?"  Jack dropped to the surface of the land, standing infront of the leader of the Assassins.

**CHAPTER 28**


**MACHINES**

**VS**

**JACK AND MANNY**


"Dude, remember when the Assassins broke into the Rotunda in Mothers House?" Jack leaned over and waited for Manny to respond.

"Yeah, Dogs, right?"  Manny looked at Jack.

"Walking Dogs, upright like us. Take a look at them now."  Jack and Manny watched from a distance as the Assassin Dogs were changing from four legged Animals to monster's, standing 10 feet tall.  The Assassins were no longer Dogs.  Their bodies convulsed from the outside in, exposing the Creatures bodily innards.

"Dude, the Wolves are no longer wolves, they're Monster-Wolves Jack. Monsters dude, that walk and maybe talk like us." Manny sighed.

The Leader of the Assassins moved rapidly to stop Jack and Manny from escaping to the Tunnels in the Alter World, trying to return to the Rotunda below.

"Jack, what are these things?"  Manny sighed.

"They have the ability to morph into other forms." Jack sighed.  " Monster Creatures Manny, Okay?"

"Dude, these aren't animals' bro they're Huge Werewolf-like creatures, giant, fucking Werewolf Creatures Jack." Manny was still coughing, unable to catch his breath.

Jack looked at Manny who was trying to digest what Jack told him.

"They look real hungry Jack....Like, they're salivating and they're heading in our direction."  Manny coughed again, with vomit in this throat.

"It's time to take a stand, give me a few seeds." Jack ordered Manny.

"Huh...You want more seeds, Bro?"  Manny continued coughing, having a hard time breating.

"Here we go again. What're you gonna do Jack?"  Manny watched Jack approach the lead Were-Wolf, with the seeds in his hand.

"I'm gonna feed this Bustard his treats. A few seeds Manny...Stand back bro..."

"Jack threw a hand full of seeds at the lead Wolf, some of which entered the nose and mouth of the Beast.

Jack ran back to Manny.  The two newly appointed Guardians by Mother, watched the seeds starting to germinate instantly inside the

Wolf Pack leader, ripping its body from a Dog like Creature of the Dark, to a Creature never seen in this World before this day.

Manny and Jack were caught off guard as the leader of the Wolf Pack morphed into an Alien kinda Monster, scaring both Jack and Manny beyond their confines of Humanity.

"Dude...walk slowly...don't talk, just slowly follow me...no questions..." Jack quietly directed Manny to follow him away from the creature which was transitioning from Dog to a Giant, Black killing Machine.

"Jack, this thing is morphing again, into something I've have never seen before, in my life.  We gotta get outa here Jack."

"Calm down Dude. Breathe buddy...don't say a word...just follow me quietly and don't draw attention to what's happening to the Wolves." Jack sighed.

"Bra. This lead Creature is morphing into something really bad...The other packs of animals are eating the Leaders excised bodily flesh, engulfing the seeds and spreading them throughout the Wolf Pack.  The ingested seeds are exposing the innards of the creatures body."  Manny had begun vomiting the crud that had welled up in his throat.

"The seeds are germinating inside all of the rest of the creature's bodies.  These things, these anomalistic created Creatures are about to explode Bro." Jack warned Manny.  "Come on...continue walking quietly.  We gotta get outa here NOW." Jack helped Manny through the tunnel leading to the Rotunda below.

The other Wolves were beginning to change into resurrected Creatures like their leader. The Fold swallowed the seeds, causing the excised bodily flesh of their Leader to turn Black.  Manny did as Jack told him. Both Guardians put distance between themselves and the Assassins as fast as their legs could carry them.

"What's happening Jack?"  Manny was winded from running away from the Wolf Pack before it exploded.

The two Guardian Cop's left the Wolves who were transitioning from Dog to Monsters.  Monster of an unknown breed of killer dog.

"The Assassins ate the seeded flesh that was ingested by their leaders. The seeds will immediately begin germinating inside the 1000 Pack of Wolves. Their stomachs are starting to burst."  Jack and Manny continued running away from the Wolf Pack, before the indigestion in the stomachs of the Wolves became a bomb ready to explode.

The Wolves had begun growing exponentially within seconds of ingesting the Seeds.  The explosion was seconds away from happening.

"We gotta go Manny.  Come on, 'let's get back to the Rotunda below.'' The answer to eliminating the recreated Monsters will be found in the Rotunda. "Jack and Manny headed back down the tunnel to the Rotunda, hoping to find Mother.  Most of Mothers Sentinels had been slain by the Creatures from the Dark side of hell.

1000 Werewolves were able to separate from their original bodily forms, creating identical replicas of themselves.  This anomaly continued repeating itself as the Monster population expanded exponently.  The Co-existence of these new breeds were altering egos of the original Werewolf's,  feeding on one another.  Confusion, retaliation, and self-destruction was the ammunition used by the Monsters against themselves.

Jack and Manny were now on the right track.  Returning back to the Rotunda to find most of the Sentinels dead.  Jack and Manny needed to seed the Dead, resurrect the Sentinels in a new and renewed life form. Mother was still absent, gone. Jack and Manny could only hope for her immediate return.

Getting back down the Tunnel to the Rotunda was fraught with despair. No more seeds were available.  Mother was nowhere in sight and the two travelers were left inside the empty walls of the Rotunda, facing a far worse adversary waiting for them.

**CHAPTER 29**

**THE DEATH OF TIME**

"Jack, I don't wanna make a thing about the Attack that's about to call out our number, but, watch closely at these newly created Monsters. They're not real Jack, there Machines."  Manny sighed, looking at his friend for a response.

"Geeze, you might be right Manny.  Evidently the Dogs, after turning into Werewolves, were and are really, Machines.  How could this happen bro?"  Jack sighed.

"They somehow were able to self-transformation from Animal to a sophisticated Machine?  Are they Robots dude?"  Jack coughed..."Please tell me that the Werewolves are not Machines or Robots."

"Jack...Everything in the Alter World is in Crazy mode.  Everything is changing...everything is morphing into whatever these Creatures are going to become.  I think giving the seeds to the creatures put them over the cliff."  Manny winced.

"Bro, whatever is happening here is not going to end well...we need to get top side and get help, if that's possible."  Jack's options were limited and useless.

"Dude, maybe the Seeds the Werewolves ingested, turned them into Mechanical-Creatures, Machines.  You think they can talk?"  Manny was curious.

"Manny, this new version of the Dogs that we first came in contact with, no longer exists.  You're right as rain.  The new generation of Animals...or whatever they are, Machines, have the ability of self-regeneration.  They're living material, morphing into Machines....which is impossible."  Jack sighed...A Machine can't be living Cells...'

"We need to get outa here now Manny...Everything these Machines are doing is somehow controlled by someone or something we can't see or feel.  We gotta get the hell out of here buddy."  Jack cried, turning and spotting the Black Menace, the First sight of the Machines.

"It's impossible Jack." Manny was distraught, his whole life lay before his eyes. "We're doomed Bro. There's no way outa this Alter World, without being seen by the Machines.  It's too late for us Jack."

"Bro, stop it. We're too old to be losers.  We can't give up the fight Manny."  Jack consoled his best friend.

Jack and Manny tried to keep their wits about them, while still hiding in the confines of the Rotunda.  The two continued watching the Machine-like Creatures Evolving from Animals to a Giant Black Death...killing Machines.

The Sentinels were erased by the Machines. Their bodies were strewn into the winds of time   Mother was nowhere to be found. She just disappeared from existence.  Jack and Manny now had an impossible task. How to save their souls without losing their lives.

The Mechanical Beasts had occupied most of the Rotunda, not noticing that two old Cops were hidden inside the Rotunda's Holy room.  The One room where Mother had been Born.

Inside the confines of the Holy Throne, Manny and Jack lay hidden in a secret conclave.  The Rotunda was alive with Creatures of the Dark side, fighting among themselves, without rhyme or reason.  The creatures seemed to be missing a leader to organize them.  This was a lucky break for Jack and Manny.

The two Cop's waited quietly inside the Holy Room of the Rotunda, hoping for the Return of Mother to set them free and win the battle with the Machines.

 The Seeded Machines were preparing to return to the streets above, to their new World.   The Machines set the Rotunda on fire, then left the Alter World, going topside to continue their devastation of the Humans. All existing forms of life were at risk of Death. The Battle wasn't over, it was just beginning.

Jack and Manny waited for an intervention by Mother, who had not yet returned to the Rotunda.  All hope was lost for Jack and Manny, as the fire inside the Rotunda was spreading rapidly throughout the many structures.

Jack and Manny were still hiding, waiting for the Machines to leave the Rotunda so they could escape to the streets above without being seen.

The Rotunda was all smoke, drastically affecting the two friends who were still in waiting for their moment to escape the fire and return topside.

The Two Cops needed to escape the Rotunda, but a few of the Machines were still searching the Rooms for Souls.  The temperature was risings.  The Majority of the Machines had already left the Rotunda and were moving through the tunnels to the surface of the Earth to continue the fight.

If Mother doesn't return soon, all will be lost.  Jack and Manny will die in the flames. The fire was raging out of Control.  The Alter World was in jeopardy of being eliminated. The cards for the two Cop's had been dwelt.

**CHAPTER 30**

**ESCAPE TOPSIDE**

"Jack, the fire's growing exponentially.  All access points are in flames. We're done for partner."  Manny sighed, still not able to breathe well.

"I think the Machines have left the Rotunda.  The only place that isn't burning is the Holy Room, Mothers Home."  Jack looked at his friend who was choking from the smoke that had filled the Rotunda.

"Manny, we need to get to MOTHERS HOLY ROOM.  We can wait out the fire inside her private chambers."  Jack walked over to Manny's side, put his right arm around Manny, lifting him up off the floor.

"Where we going Jack?"  Manny sighed, out of breath.

"To Mothers Holy of Holy's Buddy.  We'll let the fire burn itself out then head for the tunnel.  The Machines probably have gone topside by now. We should be okay pal."  Jack patted his best friend on his head.

"The fire Jack, it's still burning down the Rotunda.  We can't get out. We're gonna die Jack."  Manny sighed, spitting up blood from his lungs.

"It's gonna be okay pal. The fire can't get inside Mothers Holy place. Just try to relax...it won't be much longer and we can head to the tunnel, go top side and take you to a doctor." Jack lied to his friend. There are no Doctors who can cure Manny's problem.

"Jack, we've been friends since we're kids.  I remember coming to your 10th Birthday party.  My Mom and Dad had no money to buy you a gift so they took a pair of my socks and make a smiley face on the end.  I played with this sock puppet til I got married to Tuesday...Remember?"

"Yeah, I remember.  Any time you were sad, you'd grab that sock puppet and talk to it for hours.  By the way, did you ever give the puppet a name?"  Jack smiled at Manny, trying to keep him passive.

"Yeah, I named the Puppet...Jack.  Can you believe it?  I still have the Sock in my drawer in my room Jack."  Manny was coughing up more blood, closing his eyes intermittingly.

"Manny, remember the Magician who did magic tricks at my Birthday party...this guy did a trick by entering a tall oblong box, covered by a robe.  The Magician's assistant told all of us kids to say the magic word.  Remember? Manny closed his eyes and slept while Jack finished the Story.

"Anyhow...the Magician's assistant told all of us kids to say the magic word and the Magician will disappear.  I think the magic word was alakazam or something like that.  You remember Manny?"

Manny opened his eyes, looked at Jack with a slight smile on his face."  I remember.  The Magician disappeared from inside the box, right?"

"Yeah, then what happened Manny?"  Jack kept talking to his friend to keep him involved in the story, to forget the fire surrounding them.

"The Magician appeared across the room from the box, right?"  Manny was starting to relax and breathe a little better.

"What a trick, huh. This Magician was good. I wish we had a box like that, here, now."

"Well, there's a door on the other side of Mothers room and it has a robe hanging on the door.  Shall we play the game one more time Manny?"

Jack stood up and walked over to the door.  "Hey Bro, look at me...I'm gonna open this door and enter inside this box and disappear. Okay, just like the Magician did at my Birthday Party.  But you have to say the Magic word. ALACAZAM, okay. watch me Manny, I'M entering the room. I'm gonna disappear, watch me. You Ready...Say the Word Manny."

Manny sat up, then went to his knees, then stood up infront of the Magicians Door that Jack just entered.  "Manny...say the word and make me disappear."  Jack yelled from inside the tall closet.

"Jack, I don't want you to disappear.  We were kids then, 10-year-old kids. There's no magic here Jack.  We're gonna die in the fire."

"Say the magic word...make me disappear Manny."  Jack prodded his friend to play the game.

"Sure Jack. Ah, Alacazammmm."  Manny yelled, spitting up more blood.

"Jack...come on...the game is over...we're not 10-years-old any more...come out of the box." Manny was getting pissed that JACK was a jerk with no feelings for his friend.

One shoe flew from inside the box, hitting Manny in the shin. In a few seconds another shoe flew from the closet, hitting Manny on his other shin.

"Cut it out Jack, it hurts."  Manny rubbed both shins, then looked at the door to the room that Jack was inside of.  "Come out Jack, the fire is at our door.  It's over buddy. We did our best and lost the game.  Come out Jack."

Manny walked over to the door, removed the curtain.  The small closet room was empty, except for a sock laying on the floor inside the room.  The sock had a smiley face on it, and a name written on the sock.  This time the name was different. The name on Manny's sock read MOTHER.

# CHAPTER 31

## MOTHER RETURNS

"Hey Jack, why did you write Mother on the sock?"  Manny sighed. "Alacazammmm....yeah man, I remember the sock and your Birthday Party.  I used to wonder what happened to the guys on our street, like Johnny Moore, Howie Munger, Marshall Stallion and Butchie Benson....wow...those were good days."  Manny held the sock in his hands as something in the shadows of the closet began moving and it wasn't Jack.

"Hey Bro, knock it off." Manny walked over to the open door and peered inside.  A large hand grabbed Manny and pulled him inside the closet, shutting the door behind him.

"Manny, follow me." a voice in the darkness of the closet ordered Manny to comply.

"Who are you, a Machine?" Manny sighed.  "Let me go…" Alacazammmm. "Manny tried everything to get loose from whatever it was that held him in the darkness, while he continued invoking the Magicians magic word, to no avail.

"Relax, I'm taking you to a safe place where the fire cannot hurt you."

"Who are you?  Are you invisible like MOTHER?" Manny sighed, not wanting to continue the conversation.

"I'm Rosha.  I'm one of Mothers Royal Guards.  Mother is on the way here to save your life." Rosha smiled.  The pure white teeth of this invader in the closet were the only thing that could be seen in the darkness, when he smiled.

"You must come with me now.  The fire is consuming everything here in the Alter World.  Your friend, Jack Burton, it already topside waiting for you.  Come, we must leave Mothers Home before it's too late.  We will be consumed in the fire.  We don't leave Mothers Holy place." Rosha smiled.

Rosha looked at Manny with disdain. "Who is this person you are calling Alacazammmm?""It's kinda hard to explain."  Manny smiled at his protector.

"Mother is waiting for us...are you ready to morph to the streets above. The Machines have taken over the Planet." Rosha warned Manny

"So, where are you taking me."  Manny sighed.

"To another World where peace and tranquility rule all who wish to receive the wonders of existence."  Rosha asked Manny if he was ready to receive all that can be imagined, desired, freely.

"Before we go to this new World, where's my friend Jack Burton?" Manny asked Rosha.

"Your friend, Jack Burton, is already in this new world.  Come with me now, the fire is too hot to sustain our life forces here."  Rosha handed Manny the sock he found on the floor of the closet.

"Does this old sock belong to you?" Rosha smiled at Manny.

"This is my puppet that I gave Jack on his 10th Birthday.  When Jack and I were 10 years old."

"Does this symbolize something you humans need or want in your lives?  A sock with a face on it?"  Rosha and Manny were ready to morphing from the Rotunda to a world laced in flowers, Jasmine odors, Beautiful heavenly sky's, rivers scattered throughout this new land with Mountains so tall that they poked through the clouds beyond time.

"Is Jack here?"  Manny asked Rosha.

"Soon, in time your friend will come to be with you.  This is your time to be healed, to be free of the Machines.  Come, let me show you the house that has been prepared for you."

Rosha and Manny were standing infront of a house that was identical to the home that Manny grew up in.  The house was set on grasslands that were edged by a soft flowing river, etched by high purple mountains.  The front door to the home was standing open with two persons waving at Manny to enter.

"Ah....what's happening here?  I see my mother and Father waving for me to come home.  This is not real, just an illusion, right?"  Manny sighed

"Manny, you are here to heal...this is your home, these are your loved ones.  Come inside. Feel the warmth and love of your existence.

"How is this possible...my parents died years ago.  Am I dead Rosha?"

"Manny, no one ever dies.  A moment in time, here in this place, will keep your fondest memories of your life and the ones you love and the ones who loved you.   Being home is the greatest gift one can receive. Your loved ones have been waiting for you for quite some time Manny.

I must go now for a time, but will return to check in on you and your family.  Um, the odor of Jasmine.  It is so delightful, Manny...so beautiful.  I have to go now." Rosha smiled, beginning to morph into space, where emptiness erases all voids.

"Whoa...Rosha...where is Jack Burton?  Is he alive?"  Manny asked Rosha.

"Jack is not ready to come home yet.  He is fighting the good fight against the Machines.  Soon that battle, like all battles, will end and life will reconstruct itself.  All that is important and pertinent.... right now...is for you to enter your home and use your time wisely with your mother and Father.  They're waiting for you." Rosha smiled.

"Rosha, I'm dead...right...I mean...my lungs are no longer bleeding, my body has no more pain.  I must be dead...right Rosha?

"So, I'm gonna exist in this beautiful land, this place with my mother and Father... given to me by God himself...but it's not real...is it, Rosha?"  Manny sighed, frowning, confused.

"You wish to return to the place that had taken your memories, and now your life?" Rosha frowned.  "You are a strange creature.  You know that death is waiting for you in the Streets above this Alter World.  I cannot help you if you wish to return." Rosha looked at Manny, confused and dismayed.  "What is your wish, Manny Gonzales?"

" I wish to return to the World above the Alter World, right now.  I need to help save the living and heal the dead.  Jack Burton and I were about to morph to the streets above us, and fight the Machines.  That's where I wish to be Rosha."  Manny was adament.

"Then let it be so."  Rosha sighed.  "There are no returns in this place you have left.  You will continue with the pain that ails your body until it finally destroys you.  Only darkness will accept your existence.  Is this what you really desire Manny Gonzales?"  Rosha gave Manny one more chance to accept his fate in a place unknown to the living, yet occupied by the Dead.

Manny was morphed back inside the Secret room of MOTHER.  The fire had already broken through the door, the walls, the ceilings of the Holy room.

"Manny, here, swallow this seed. Hurry."  Jack ordered Manny to do as he asked.  "Swallow the seed and you'll be healed buddy."

"Jack, is it really you?"  Manny sighed.

"Yeah bro... what's wrong with you?"  Jack looked at Manny who had tears in his eyes.

"Swallow the seed and let's go top side to fight the Machines, okay buddy."  Jack gave Manny one seed of life and made him swallow it. Manny was instantly healed.  It was time to deal with the inevitable...the Machines.

**CHAPTER 32**

**THE MACHINES**

"Dude, do you remember the warehouse where all of this shit started?" Manny looked at Jack for an answer.

"Yeah bro.  The Dogs that fought the Black Menace."  Jack smiled, remembering their first battle together.

"Yeah, then came the transformation, right?  The Dogs evolved into Wolves, then Werewolves...I still believe that some unknown force was watching us from outside our Warehouse.  Someone waiting to control the 1000 killer Wolves.  What was it...remember...a shadow that stayed hidden until it was time for the Holicost...remember Jack....You called this creature the Black Menace...remember." Manny's pains were returning.  The Seed Jack gave Manny was finally working, rapidly healing Manny.

"Yeah, and the almighty Assassins.  The whole concoction of shit was because of the Assassins, right?  So how did that work out?"  Jack sighed, angry.

"Jack, We almost died at the hands of the Assassins, the Beasts of the Alter World.  Thats what I remember Bro."

Manny consumed the Seed of Life.  His body healing rapidly.

"Wow bro, this seed shit is amazing. I can feel every part of my body returning to normal and more.  Jack, I feel like a million dollars." Manny looked at Jack. "I'm getting strong dude...really strong." Manny smiled, liking his newly reconstructed body.

"Reminiscing is bad medicine Manny.  The game isn't over.  The threat to both of us getting buried in a pile of shit is close to happening." Jack didn't hold back his feelings.

"Look. The Giant, malicious Werewolves are gone...Armageddon is between us and the Machines now.  That's our reality. "Jack looked at Manny.

"Can't we just cut and run.  The Machines rule the Planet, right." Manny frowned. "Two of us against Millions of MacInnes? No way, Jack."

"Cut and run...huh.   I wish it was that easy Manny.  There's no place to run.  MOTHER has left the fight to us, just the two of us." Jack took a look around the streets hearing the clanking sounds of the Machines heading in their direction.

"Well, we still have one bag of Seeds left.  Here, take some of the seeds."  Manny opened the plastic bag holding the Seeds of Life in his hands.

"So, this is our weapon, right...the Seeds." Manny sighed.  "I hope the seeds can destroy Metal, because the Machines are heading in our direction, rapidly and they don't look happy."

"Bro, there's too many Machines to fight. We only have enough Seeds to slow them down."  Jack held his seeds cupped in his hands, ready to throw at the Machines who were rounding the street, now facing the two Detectives.

"So we just give up?  Then what?"  Manny sighed.  "Jack, we fight to the end, remember?"

"Manny, there's no end for us, only darkness in a hole, dead. Not even buried, Bro." Jack sighed.

"Jack, I visited a place where life is good.  I saw my mom and Dad in our old house, waiting for me.  A guy name Rosha took me to this place and he said he could do the same for you, if you wish it so."

"The Machines are a few feet from us Manny.  Our destiny, Fate or whatever it is, has come for us.  I'm gonna fight them Bro to my last breath."  Jack held the seeds in his hand, ready to throw the seeds into the mass of the raging Machines.

Manny was thrown into cage by the Machines. Jack was swinging his machete in all directions, destroying as many of the Machines as possible. With his last breath, Jack yelled for MOTHER to save him and Manny.

The World began spinning with a force that had grown exponentially in seconds, after Jack threw the Seeds of Life into the center of the Machines.

Manny watched as Jack was suddenly removed from the fight, rising into the clouds above the Holicost. The Machines on the ground began folding, breaking into pieces of raw metal, their bodies turning into piles of rubble, nuts and bolts.

The lock on the cage that held Manny, melted.  Manny was able to exit the cage, watching most of the Machine's dissolve into dust, before his eyes.

Manny started to exit his confines, while the  Machines were still watching him closely.  What was left of the Machines was still formidable.  The fight was not over.

"Manny, do not exit the cage.  You'll be safe there for now.  Use your seeds to protect yourself.  I'm with MOTHER. "Jack yelled to Manny through the clouds of Heaven.

"Jack, come and get me Bro. The Machines have surrounded me.  I think they're gonna kill me, Jack."  Manny was anxious to leave the cage and follow Jack and MOTHER.

"What's happening Jack...everything here on the ground is collasping into a giant hole.  Come and get me buddy...hurry...save me." Manny cried, searching the Heavens to see where Jack and MOTHER had gone.

 The heavens above, where Jack and MOTHER were overlooking the demise of the Machines and Manny, were illuminating the skies with bolts of lightning.

"Dude, we're coming...hang on.  There's still a massive number of Machines that need to be destroyed.  Hide your face, your eyes. MOTHER is sending a flash of light to erase the rest of the Machines. We're on our way Buddy."  Jack yelled to Manny from the Heavens above.

Manny did as he was told.  Still inside the Machines cage, Manny covered his face to avert the lighting strikes.  The final blast eliminated the rest of the Machines.  Manny was the only being surviving the blast of lightning.  The Machines were erased.

Jack descended back to Earth, standing infront of the cage that had held Manny imprisoned. "Hey Bro, you, okay?"  Jack opened the gate of the Cage, waving for Manny to come out.

"Is it over?"  Manny looked at Jack.

"Yeah. Somewhat. There's still a remnant of Machines out there that want to take over the World."  Jack helped Manny out of the Cage, where the two looked at one another in dismay.

 "So, we're safe now, right?"  Manny looked at Jack.

Hidden behind a three-story building, were the remnants that Jack mentioned to Manny.  100 or more Machines were regrouping for a final battle over who rules the World.  Jack and Manny made their way secretly to the building that the machines were hiding behind.

"Jack, the Machines are planning a final, all out, attack on us.  What do we do bro?" Manny sighed.

"We stand back and let MOTHER finish this War, once and for all."  Jack looked down the street, seeing 4 or 5 Machines sneaking towards their hiding place.

"Bro... we got company."  Manny sighed.

"Hide your face now.... MOTHER will send another electrical blast and eliminate the few Machines left.  Close you eyes."

MOTHER sent another electrical blast solely directed at the Machines. The Blast covered the whole area of Los Angeles.  The last few Machines were erased.  The War was over.

**CHAPTER 33**


**MOTHER RETURNS**


"Jack...can I open my eyes now?"  Manny was wondering if the Earth still existed.

"Manny, the War's over.  Problem is, all of Mankind has been infected with a virus caused by a bad Seed of Life.  The lightning strikes enhanced the power of the Seed, spreading the Virus throughout Los Angeles.  We've unknowingly created a Pandemic."  Jack was weighing their options.

"So, bring MOTHER to the streets and cancel out the Virus."  Manny sighed.

"MOTHER is already here with us now. She's cleansing the area, showering the roads, buildings and more for those still living and infected with the Virus.

We need to find a safe place and wait out MOTHER'S actions.  The whole area will be quaranted."  Jack explained to Manny.

"How's a virus created, from MOTHER sending bolts of lightning on Los Angeles?"  Manny sighed, confused.

"I don't know Bro.  Something about a bad seed being enhanced by the lighting strikes. Right now we gotta return to our Warehouse, seal the windows and doors and let MOTHER kill the VIRUS before the World becomes dead.  Like real dead." Jack was hopeful, Manny was worried.

MOTHER descended to the surface of the Earth, then disappeared deep into the core of the Planet, where her Rotunda once existed.  The fire had consumed all forms life in this Alter World.

Bodies were strewn throughout the Rotunda, caught in the flames and destruction of the Alter World's collapse.  The Earth's Crust was beginning to falter from the intense heat of the magma, destroying the bond that held the core in tack.

MOTHER searched through the rubble, looking for the original Seed of life.  Rosha was waiting for Mother to return from inside the Alter World.

Rosha needed to help Mother secure the Rotunda, then find the Original Seed of Life.

The Seed, hopefully survived the fire.   The Rotunda was laying in piles of rubble. Scorched body parts were welded to the floor of the Rotunda, in skeletal form.  The body parts came from the Death of MOTHERS Sentinels and Guardians, with some of the Assassins included.

The flames had burned off the flesh of the Sentinels, leaving their lifeless bones bonded to the Structures of the Rotunda.  Bodily Ash covered the floor of the Rotunda.  Only Rosha and MOTHER lived through the disaster, barely alive after the Holicost ended.

"Rosha...we need to find the Seed before the core of the Earth separates and Earth collapses.  Take a look through the Rotunda for my Sentinels...Perhaps a few of our Soldiers survived the fire to help us."  MOTHER directed Rosha.

"Yes Mother.  There is one other that has survived the fire.  A Human.  I gave him one of the last few seeds, to heal him.  Later, Unfortunately, the seed I gave him was infected with a virus.  This Human was the only survivor found in the Rotunda, besides me.  The Human is now top side and will need help soon.  He is the friend of Jack Burton." Rosha was concerned.

"The virus will spread to other living entities above the streets, if not already done so."  MOTHER SIGHED.

Time was not on the side of MOTHER and Rosha.  Earth's inner core was not holding...Earth was beginning to break apart.  The Earth's Core was Seconds from failing.

Mountains began crumbling throughout the World.  Oceans were rising.  200 mile an hour winds were ravaging the surface of Planet.  What life forms that existed on Earth's surface were insects, snakes, and one dubious Creature referred to as the Black Menace.  Armageddon was not over, yet.

The inner walls of the Earth were collasping.  The outer Core was also crumbling, allowing the inner core filling with molten magma, rising up through the Crust, extruding it's liquified Stone to the surface of the Earth.

"Rosha, we need to seal the Inner and outer Core to keep the Earth from collasping.  The Earth will implode if not put in check."  MOTHER sighed.

"Rosha, if this Planet bursts, the explosion will throw all of the other 8 Planets in this Solar System into chaos.  The Solar System will break free from the Sun's gravitational pull, spinning all eight planets into the darkness of Space, including what's left of Earth."

MOTHER was trying to stop the inevitable. Total destruction.  The Solar system was beginning to collapse alongside Earth.  All nine Planets will be erased if Earth is not seated in its orbit.

"We must stop the Cores from collasping Rosha...I need you to go into the Earths Core's and seal the Cores.  We need to stop the damage, the magma flow and repair the Cores." Mother ordered Rosha.

Rosha descended into the lower crust of the Earth.  Opening a hole in the Crust allowed him to descend deeper into the Inner and outer Core where he could create a perimeter seal to plug each of the core's bleeding of magma.

Rosha's power of the four elements of life were used to manipulate the two cores from colliding with one another.

Rosha was able to seal the Cores, save the Earths Inner confines, allowing the Earth's surface to return to normal.

While Top side...MOTHER watched the destruction of the land subside, the winds ending their torment, the waters of the oceans recede too normal. Rosha had done his work.

"Rosha, let us return to the Rotunda and search for our Sentinels and Guardians.  I have enough seeds to plant inside the bodies of the lost." MOTHER SIGHED.

"Yes, and the one above that I told you about.  He is still carrying a virus.  Whatever we cure, will be undone if the Virus inside Jack Burtons friend isn't corrected."  Rosha was adamant to get started.

The search for Manny was on the list of Rosha's findings.  Rosha needed to confine the Virus that was growing exponentially inside Manny's body. Rosha's problems were just beginning.  Manny was nowhere to be found.

Jack was waiting for Rosha to make his way topside to remove the infected Seed of life out of Manny's body.  Everyone was waiting for the return of Manny Gonzales.

**CHAPTER 34**

# THE END HAS COME

The Earth was settling back into its orbit.  The Planet was still in pain.  If Jack and Rosha cannot find Manny, a worldwide Pandemic will ensue.

"Jack, I thought Manny was with you?"  Rosha sighed, feeling the pain of defeat.

"Rosha, Manny was here a few minutes ago. He left to use the bathroom."  Jack looked at Rosha with confusion.  "What's the problem...a quick pee and Manny will return...okay?"

"Where is this friend of yours?" Rosha looked at Jack, panic stricken.  "We need to find your buddy and restrain him from talking, touching or seeing other life forms, or the world will fall into a powerful and deadly Viral Pandemic."

"Look, I told you that Manny was taking a piss.  He'll be right back, relax."  Jack was starting to believe that Manny was a walking time bomb.

"Jack, where is the bathroom. We can't wait any longer for him to return.  It takes one other person to come in contact with Manny and the Virus will speed among Millions instantly."  Rosha sighed.  "Take me to the Bathroom...now."

The bathroom was a short distance from where Jack and Rosha were waiting for Manny. A quick walk to the bathroom, subdue Manny and return to the Rotunda to keep Manny away from other Humans was the number one priority on the menu.

"Hey Rosha, what's up?"  Manny was at the urinal, relieving his kidneys.

"Manny, you need to come with me to the Rotunda...Now."  Rosha warned Manny.  "Manny, I'm so sorry."

"What're you talking about Rosha?  Sorry for what?"  Manny zipped up his pants, turned to wash his hands when he saw his face in the mirror on the wall of the Bathroom.

"What the hell...Manny looked at Rosha.  What's happening to me Rosha?"  Manny held his breath, feeling dizzy.

"Here, let me help you...we need to return to the Rotunda now. Okay Manny?  You have an infection and Mother will have to cure you...okay?" Rosha sighed again.

Rosha caught Manny in his arms.  Manny passed out and was falling face first to the cement floor of the Bathroom.

"Jack, come over here and help me.  Manny passed out on the floor." Rosha yelled to Jack. "Help me pick him up."

"What happened to Manny Rosha?"  Jack stooped down to wake his friend. "Rosha, is Manny infected?  The skin on his face and arms looks like Snake skin...What's happening to him?"

"We need to carry Manny back down the tunnels to the Rotunda.  He ingulfed a virus from one of the seeds I gave him.  The Virus is changing his DNA."  Rosha sighed.

"Okay....let's get down to the Rotunda.  Is Mother there?  Can she cure Manny from the altered DNA he's exhibiting?"  Jack helped Rosha carry Manny through the secret tunnel to the burned-out Rotunda Below.  Mother was waiting for them.

"Hurry, put your friend on this table.  I need to take a sample of Manny's DNA before we operate on him."  Mother directed Rosha to wash his hands, change his clothes and prepare the operating table for surgery.

"Ah...Manny is still unconscious.  This isn't good, is it?"  Jack sighed.

Manny's skin was changing from a normal human to an all-out snake skin.  The snake skin had transformed the insides of Manny's body, changing his DNA from Human to Serpent. Manny's face, arms and legs were reformed to that of a full body Anaconda. With luck, Manny's mind will continue to functioned normally.  He can talk, swallow and eat anything that catches his eye, including Rosha and Jack.

"Manny, do you feel pain? Mother asked him.

"MOTHER....you came to help me?"  Manny hissed," his body still in a morph condition from Human to Snake.

"I feel wierd Mother.  The words inside my mouth are slithering off of my tongue.  My arms, legs...my whole body is covered with this snake skin...what's happening to me?"

Manny climbed up on the operating table, curled up in a circle, lunging at Rosha and Jack.  Mother was still invisible.

"Wow dude.  You...ah...look different bro... really different."  Jack looked at Manny's cat eyes.  "Still feeling pain pal?"

"No Jack, there is no more pain.... I feel like a God."  Manny raised up, looking at Jack and Rosha. His Anaconda body had begun healing, not as a human, rather a beast of a Snake.  Manny slithered from the table and exited the Rotunda to the street, top-side.

"Whoa....hold on Bud...you're in no condition to be testing the tunnels again.  You should rest...okay?" Jack frowned.

"Rest?,  when my body feels the power of the Snake.  NO....I'm taking the tunnel to the streets above, now.  I need to see the Sun light, other people and other animals.  I need to see everything Jack. I'm HUNGRY."

"Rosha, now what?"  Jack was out of ideas.

"ONLY ONE OPTION" MOTHER SIGHED." We need to follow Manny to the streets above. He's already inside the tunnel, heading rapidly to the surface of the streets."

"He's gonna try to interface with the living.... Manny has been altered." Rosha frowned.  "Your friend is gaining size, shape and the power of the Serpent.  Mother needs to deal with Manny.  I'm not strong enough to fight the Serpent side of Manny. " Rosha sighed, "We need Mother to step up and put the Snake to sleep."  Jack sighed, "Put Manny to sleep, or kill him?"  Jack was angry, feeling helpless.

"Rosha...look at Manny's face...his head is changing again.  He's morphed into a super-sized Anaconda.  Rosha, you and I cannot take Manny down. We need Mother and a few others to secure him for the upcoming surgery." Jack looked at Rosha.

"This isn't right." Rosha sighed. "Manny is moving through the tunnel at light speed.  We can't catch up with him before he reaches the living top side.  More Humans will die by the Virus or the bite of the Snake, whichever comes first.

"Rosha... Jack...Manny is in need of feeding.  Those Humans still existing top side are in danger, a terrible danger.  It's impossible to intercede and stop Manny. When Manny reaches the streets above, his first instinct is to eat.  And believe me boys, he's gonna eat.

## CHAPTER 35


## THE DAY OF THE SERPENT


"Rosha, Jack, we need to morph top side...now...Manny will be there in a few minutes.  I'll morph you two to the streets above.  We need to stop Manny from filling his gullet with Human or Animal flesh. The killing must stop now."  Mother sighed.

It's time. Stand with me."   Mother stood firm, to save the innocent existing top side from Manny. The newly created Anaconda was indeed, Hungry and out of control.

MOTHER prepared Rosha and Jack to morph to the streets above, find Manny and subdue him. Mother was preparing a DNA VILE she mixed, to reverse Manny's condition.  This special vile, when injected into Manny, will put him to sleep, temporarily.   When Rosha and Jack arrive top side, they will immediately be faced with the Monster, Manny has become.... The sleeping Giant.

"MOTHER is on her way to prepare a vile that will kill the other two DNA's in Manny's body. Manny, or whatever he is now, is staring at both of us, drooling." Jack sighed.

"Mother better Hussle.  Manny is intermittingly changing shapes from one DNA to the other, then the other.  There's no way we can hold him or it, at bay.  He's too large and beyond powerful. Too powerful."

Rosha was checking his watch every two seconds, waiting for Mother to arrive, with the mixture of three DNA'S inside a Vile.  If the vile works, two of the creatures existing inside Manny's body will be removed, returning Manny back to normal.  At least that was the thought, if not the hope.

"MOTHER filled her Vile with all three DNA's. Mother called upon the wind to morph her top side where Rosha and Jack were waiting for her. Jack and Rosha were knee deep in Trying to put a giant Anaconda to sleep, with no luck.

"I hear the wind coming towards us. It has to be MOTHER.  I hope she knows what she's doing?"  Rosha frowned.

" Buckle up Bro, we still have to tie down this monster until Mother arrives top side." Jack rubbed his two hands together, took a deep breath, looked at Jack for a quick second.  'Ready buddy, The Monster is across the street from us...time to tie this bastard down so Motter can inject him with her DNA mix.  Let's go."

Rosha and Jack took to the streets, crossing over to the other side of the street where Manny, the Serpent, was waiting for them.

"Jack, the second mutant seed that was given Manny should have turned him back to normal." Rosha paused before making contact with the Monster.

"Jack, the creature residing inside the body of your friend is staring at us.  If Mother destroys the creature, your friend is dead." Rosha looked at Jack, tired and broken.

MOTHER arrived with the prepared vile in her hand.  Neither Rosha nor Jack could see Mother, just the vile she was carrying.

"Guys, we'll have to approach Manny.  In a few seconds we will know if he is amenable to deal with us.  We need to be ready with this new seed of Life to inject into the Serpents body."

Mother had prepared a cure to remove the "Serpent DNA" from Manny's Body.  If the DNA blend that mother made works, the Serpent DNA will be removed. If the mix in the vile doesn't work, Manny will most likely transform over and over again, into something never seen before on Earth.

Mothers Magic compounds are blended with the injection of a new Seed of Life.  Manny's DNA should immediately return him to normality. Hope and Fate were the two extra tools needed to complete Manny's re-transformation back to HUMAN.

After Mother injected the antivirus DNA into Manny's body, Manny began convulsing.  His body was trying to reject his Human DNA that was ravaging his body.

The injection wasn't working as hoped.  A reaction to the Seed caused a magnetic response inside his body, destroying both DNAs inside his cell's while unknowingly creating a third DNA Mix of a Creature that none of the three could have ever imagined.

Both of Manny's Human and Serpent form were replaced with this new life form.  A creature dripping blood from its pours, missing chunks from its rancid body.  The flesh, existing on this Creatures body was turning black.  The odor of the Monster caused the three team mates to vomit, non-stop.  Manny no longer existed as Jack Burtons best friend.

Manny's newly created being, harnessed a third DNA.  Manny was nothing less than a Monster, waving about its 4 arms, 4 legs, two heads and a thousand eyes .  The three mates were stupidified, hopeless that Manny will ever return to his old self again.  This newly formed body from hell, stood watching the three amigos, waiting for them to make their move.

This monstrosity stood over 10 feet tall.  Manny looked at the three of his friends who were trying to return him to Human form.  This Creature was angered, ready to attack his old friends of the past, post haste.  The three amigos were in Manny's sights, to be destroyed by this no name Creature.

The Monster was the results of another error, Caused by MOTHERS accidental infusion of her DNA into what was left of Manny's reformed body.  Manny's Cellular Structure housed a combined mix of three DNAs into one DNA.  The mixed was reduced into a pie of cellular Mush.  Manny was a disaster, out of control, a killing machine like non other.

"Jack, Rosha, you two need to leave the area now.  It's up to me to cure Manny." MOTHER sighed.

"Mother, you gonna kill Manny?"  Jack asked Mother who was still invisible.

"I will try not to hurt him, Jack.  Saving his life or returning him to normal is nearly impossible.  He has 1 percent of his original DNA intact.  99% of his blended DNA now controls his body.  His Brain is no longer that of your friend.  I made a terrible mistake Jack, that cannot be fixed."

"Bull shit. It was you who mixed his Cells with yours and two other badly infected seeds. Now look at what you created. Get him back Mother, you owe Manny his life."  Jack was beside himself, with anger.

"Jack, I'm so sorry...I don't know what to do to help Manny.  His cells need to heal themselves.  We need to give Manny time to correct his body."  Mother sighed.   I cannot correct Manny's cellular structure.  Manny is three bodies mixed inside this Creature.  The mixed DNA is racing through his physical system like never before.  I believe, with time, Manny's DNA will correct his body and return him to Human.

"Manny's lost, gone Mother.   He doesn't know who or what he is now....MOTHER...FIX HIM." Jack looked at Rosha.

"Mother, Jack is right. You can remove the two Bad DNA's, somehow. Look at what you created Mother.  Take a look...this is our friend who helped us save what is left of the Rotunda.  He deserves better than this mother.... Fix Him...you can Fix him."

"Rosha, you are right.  I will work on saving Manny, but first, you and Jack need to incarcerate him so I can work on restricting his DNA back to Human form.  I need samples of his current DNA.  We need to see what he is currently made of now, and how we can return Manny to normal.  Okay?"  Mother looked at Jack and Rosha.

"Mother, we can take Manny to the Coroners Laboratory.  It's a short walk to the Lab. Everything is shut down there, so the Laboratory is yours to use."  Jack spoke to Mother.

"Then let's go now.  Every second is critical to returning your friend back to normal.  Let's go to the Lab now."  Mother began walking when Rosha and Jack told her to stop.

"How are we gonna transport a 10-foot-tall Monster, that's outa control, to the Coroners Lab, without raising havoc among those existing in the city.   One look at Manny's newly formed Body will frighten the community, The Police will come to stop Him, by shooting him dead, Mother.   You need to turn Manny invisible then transport him and us, to the Coroners Laboratory....got it."  Jack frowned, talking to Mother who was and is still Invisible.

"Got it Jack...prepare yourselves for a Morph to the Laboratory..." MOTHER agreed, swooping Jack, Rosha and Manny in her winds of time direct to the Coroners Laboratory.

**CHAPTER 36**

# THE CORONER'S LABORATORY

On their way to the Coroners Laboratory, inside the Morph, Rosha asked the 64,000 Dollar Question.

"Rosha, were you aware of Jacks Dream state?"  MOTHER asked Rosha.  "I have been Reading his mind.  There seems to be something drastically wrong with his thinking.  Rosha, Jack has been dreaming for years about a Creature existing below the Earth's Crust, coming up to the streets of Humanity at least once a month, to take innocents back down the  tunnel to the secret tunnel that drops below the Earth's Crust.  His dream tunnel is like the one that will take us to where this Creature exists."  MOTHER ended the morph, dropping at the entrance of the Coroners Laboratory.

"Mother, I think it's best to not bring up the dream that Jack keeps experiencing over and over again.  This will just frustrate him, which will keep us from doing what is needed in the Lab.  We need to remove the three DNA's instilled in Jacks body, return him to just the one original DNA, and bring him back to normal.  Okay...Can you do this mother?"  Rosha sighed, looking at Jack, confused, worn and torn, about to collapse into another plane of existence where his darkest fears await his arrival.

Mother went to work consciously removing the DNA of the Anaconda.  10 hours of re-arranging Jacks DNA had still not corrected his Matrix's as yet.  There was one other DNA that was still existing in the Matrix's of Jacks bodily composition...The Black Menace.  Both of the DNA's were instilled in Jacks bodily makeup from two infected Seeds of Life that Mother had unknowingly instilled into Jack's DNA.

"Mother, how's Jack doing?"  Rosha asked Mother.

"I was able to remove the Anaconda DNA successfully.  Jacks body will begin trying to return to normality.  However, the next step has to be completed if Jack is to return to his Human state of existence...the second DNA is that of the Black Menace.  Jack's DNA had melded with this DNA completely. I'm not sure if I can remove the Menace DNA without losing Jack completely.  His mind could rupture, leaving him a virtual Vegetable Rosha.  Do you wish me to continue anyhow?" Mother sighed, fearing the worse for Jacks success to live on as before, with his original DNA, intact.

The odds of Mother being able to remove the second DNA along with Jack's Matrix's and that of the Black Menace, were glued together. If Mother try's to unlock Jack's Matrix and remove the Black Menace DNA, he could become an anomaly, a non-existent entity.

"Mother, what the hell is a NON- EXISTANT."  Rosha sighed, fearing Mothers answer.

"Rosha, the two existing DNAs created a break in Jack's Matrix.  I would have to cut the entangled Black Menace DNA loose from the Human DNA of Jack Burton.  You wish me to continue with the removal." Mother frowned at Rosha.

"You've anathemized Jack heavily.  We need to act now before the anesthesia wears off."  Rosha warned Mother.

"Then I will unwind the two DNA's that are bonded with one another. You must realize that I may have to cut and tear Jack's Matrix to separate the two DNAs from one another.  Rosha, The Black Menace DNA will always linger inside the body of Jack, after the surgery."

"What does that mean Mother...Jack will not be Jack any longer or what?"  Rosha sighed.  "Explain, before you cut him."

DNA is the makeup of an individual entity, Human or not. It is beyond my knowledge how three DNAs could possibly exist inside one entity, named Jack Burton, and work." Mother cried.  "Rosha, you need to know that Jack may no longer be the Jack you knew in the past." Mother warned Rosha.

"Jack is strong...do it, cut the Black Menace from his Matrix's.  He'll survive, even if he's a little different, he'll still be Jack." Rosha knew that Jack would awaken soon, real soon, and it was now or never for Mother to do her best in restoring Burton to his old self.

Mother agreed, removing a static electric blade to untangle the two DNA's in Jack's Matrix.  If Mother is careful, Jack should be able to resume his life as before, with some small tinges or eruptions in his mind set.

The surgery was slow.  One step at a time to untangle two DNA's where only one should exist.  When Mother began surgically cutting the Black Menace DNA from the original DNA that Created Jack, a tear ripped a minor section of the strains, causing the Matrix's of both life forms to begin melding into one.

"Oh my God Rosha, the two individuals are melding into one.  It is impossible to separate the two without major damage against the holder, the body of Jack."  Mother sighed.

"What does that mean?"  Rosha hissed at Mother.

"We've solidified the DNAs into one new DNA.  Two persons inside one body."  Mother sighed.

"How is that possible?  Jack will exist as Jack and the Black Menace at the same damn time? How is that possible?  You need to separate the two persons. There has to be two bodies, not one, two. One for each DNA."  Rosha yelled at Mother for not checking the infected Seeds of Life she implanted into Jacks Matrix.

"If I continue cutting the two Matrix's apart, we may create something that has never existed in normality, in life."  Mother sighed.

"Can you find the head of the Menace DNA and diffuse it from Jacks DNA?  In other words, use the electrified blade to zap the Menace DNA, kill it if possible, and remove it carefully from Jack's Matrix?"

"It's not that easy Rosha.  There is always the risk that permeant damage will change Jack."  Mother sighed. "Two bodies are needed. You are right.  One of the two bodies needs to be vacant, dead, a container without life.  If I can separate the DNA's with little risk or damage, place the Black Menace Matrix inside the Dead Bodily shell, then energize the shell and the body. Wait and see what happens." MOTHER was finally with the program and more confident for its success.

"Okay...so we need a body, another body besides Jacks body.  A dead body will not have an Active DNA, right?"  Rosha looked at Mother with dismay.

"Rosha, a recent dead body will be needed.  We're here at the Coroners Laboratory, right?  There should be bodies interred here, to choose from.  A body that can be resurrected with the Black Menace DNA.  That is possible...however, to resurrect the DNA of the Black Menace in a lifeless body, we need to also resurrect its Matrix along with Its completed DNA. We may face negative results that may cause the illumination of all life forms on Earth.  The Black Menace will become hell on Earth Rosha, like nothing we have ever seen before." Mother went to work as discussed.

"So, we deal with the Hell on Earth later, after we resurrect Jack into himself again...if you know what I mean." Rosha was hoping for a positive response from MOTHER.

"Then let it be so...."  Mother went to work separating the two DNA's and the two Matrix's from Jack Burtons Body.  Rosha searched the interred bodies for a cadaver that could sustain and control the Black Menace, when resurrected.

Hours passed as MOTHER diligently worked to complete the plan as discussed. The transfers of the DNA and Matrix of the Black Menace was completed.  Electrical shock was next on the menu, to now, resurrect the Menace.  Jack's surgery was completed as well, with a few glitches, but basically returning him to Humanity as before.

"Rosha, stand by the Body of the Menace. It is time to resurrect this dead body."  Mother cleaned up the surgery table of Jack Burton, allowing him to rest and restore his strength.  The two surgery's went well.  The results however were yet to be realized.

**CHAPTER 37**

**THE RESURRECTION**

"Mother, are you looking at the Body lying on the table?"  Rosha sighed.  "This body is now moving.  It's alive."

"Yes Rosha, our surgery seems to be a success.  The Black Menace is alive as an individual like us."

"And....what comes next Mother?"  Rosha frowned, watching the dead man awaken.

"We'll need to be watchful.  I know little about the Black Menace.  However, the cadaver we chose is strong.  We could bind the Menace before it awakens, just in case it attempts to attack us."

"Too late Mother, your Frankenstein Monster just opened its eyes."  Rosha sighed.  "And now it's sitting up, looking directly at us."

"Humm, it is good to be inside this human form.  The darkness has been lifted and now I see the ones who resurrected me.  For that and that alone, I will let you three live one more day."

Mother didn't respond to the Menace's comment and stayed invisible, watching the actions of the Monster and its intentional actions.

"I see two Humans, yet I feel there are three.  The one who is capable of invisibility holds powers greater than mine.  Show yourself?"  The

Menace frowned, leaving the cadaver table, trying to walk over to the where Rosha and Jack were talking.

"This new body is not functioning as it should.  I cannot walk without falling.  What is happening to me?"  The Menace hissed with anger against the Invisible One...Mother.

"You are inside a mortal's cadaver, that has expired.  It will take a while for you to regulate this body to function properly.  Time will allow your new confines to correct itself and function normally."  Mother spoke for the first time to the Menace.

"Ahh...so you exposed yourself, yet still invisible...how is this possible?"  The Menace coughed, expanding the lungs of this new body.

"You're the Black Menace."  Rosha stepped backwards, behind the table that Jack was sitting on.

"And who are you little one."  The Menace smiled.

"I am Rosha, keeper of the Realm of Rotunda and Guardian of the ONE...called Mother."  Rosha stepped a few feet backwards, watching the body of the revived cadaver's eyes beginning to glow red, on fire.

"Well now, the littlest of the three can talk.  You are so proud of your position, which I will shortly remove from your body."  The Menace tried again to get his new body to function and walk towards Rosha and Jack without success.

"Damn this body...return my body to me...NOW."  The voice of the Menace echoed throughout the Laboratory, breaking windows, opening and shutting doors.

"Your body no longer exists....it has been erased.  Your abilities are shut down.  The body you exist inside of now, is broken, was dead, and now lives with you inside of it.  You and this body shall be immediately incarcerated into the confines of an impenetrable Penitentiary for the rest of your existence.  Others like yourself exist in this forbidden place, forever.  You will fit in well with the evil that resides in this place." Mother was terse.

"And where does this so-called Penitentiary exist?"  The creature sighed, fuming with anger inside its cadaver body.

"Off World."  Mother sighed.

"And how do you three think you can bind me and my powers......please...humor me."  The Menace shrugged its shoulders.

"Dude, did you see the spikes coming out of the Menace's Backside...all along his spine. He's starting to morph into his original existence." Rosha sighed.

Jack was waking up, confused, yet strong and back to his normal self.

"Rosha, this guy has to be interred in prison, like now.  It is changing into something out of this world...like right now... It is growing exponentially.  We gotta incarcerate this creature now or pay the consequences." Jack sighed.

"Mother, where is this Jail located." Rosha called upon Mother to take this creature and morph it into the Spacial Prison, forever."

"My new body is coming together...my powers are returning.  Show me this Creature called Mother now, or i will burn you two creatures into dust."  The Black Menace was now at 90 % recovered.  The Cadaver Body was resurrected.

"Mother?"  Rosha whizzed." The Black Menace has regained his abilities...like he's big now, he has powers again and is threatening to eliminate Jack and I into dust.  Can you take charge of this creep and send him in to the prison in Space...now."  Rosha sighed.

Mother didn't reply to Rosha.  The Menace laughed hideously, downplaying the value of the so-called invisible creature referred to as MOTHER.

"Well, seems this mother is unable to respond to your requests.  So... let me help you."

The Black Menace wielded the stars to descend to the Earth, take Jack and Rosha on a Disney ride into Space...never to return.

**CHAPTER 38**


**THE RIDE TO ETERNITY**


"Stop. You wish to see me, Creature, then come forward, let me show you your fate."  Mother laughed.

"Hey, I'm kinda getting used to this cadaver.  It's warm and fuzzy.  So, we will finally come face to face and see who will continue on, til the end of time."

The Menace's new body was beginning to shake uncontrolled. His new digs were detreating rapidly, his mind fumbling with unknown words. The giant cadaver body was beginning to crumble into dust.  The Black Menace was on a crash course with death.

"Mother, morph this Bastard to the Prison of the lost."  Rosha looked at Mother who was indeed, visible.

"Rosha, I cannot morph this body into Space.  The Menace's body is crumbling.  The Menace is on his last leg." Mother looked at Jack and Rosha with concern.

"Then let's send him below the Earth's Crust.  The Rotunda has been destroyed...this may be a good place for the Menace to live out his days without hurting or killing anyone." Rosha waited for Mother to respond.

"Rosha, the Rotunda is a Holy place that can never be breached.  We will never allow an Evil like the Menace to exist in our confines of peace, love and tranquility."  Mother was interrupted by Jack.

"Guys, the Menace is evaporating in the wind.  Don't we need to stop him or something?"  Jack sighed.

"Boys, the Menace has regained his powers and is testing his abilities below the Earth's Crust.  We need to stop him and end his days, now."  Mother warned Jack and Rosha to use the powers of the seeds to incarcerate the creature and return his body back inside the cadaver.

"Ah....so you understood my plan and now you three wish to send this Cadaver back into the Laboratory where it came from?  I cannot allow this to happen.  Behold...

"What the hell Jack.  What just happened to us? Where are we and how did we get here?"  Rosha sighed.  "Where's the Black Menace...where's Mother?"

"I have no idea what just happened to us.  All I know is we are not in the Rotunda or topside."  Jack was confused as well.

"Or maybe we're in limbo....in no-where land?"  Rosha sighed, helping Jack stand up, who fell to the floor of this place that seemly does not exist.

"What about Mother Rosha?  Is she still with us or not?"  Jack was having a panic attack.

"I don't think so Jack.  I think we were morphed here by the Menace.  I think the Menace and Mother have business to complete, without us being involved."

"Okay, now what?  We sit and wait in this darkness until someone comes to get us?"  Jack sighed. "That's our best bet, is to wait?"

"Yeah, I think that's what's gonna happen to us. We sit tight and wait for someone to come and get us." Rosha sighed.

"Dude, that could be a very, very, long time."  Jack swallowed his next words, trying to stay positive.

"This could be our Eternity Jack.  We gotta face facts." Rosha winced. "We need to stay positive, check things out, here in this place and find something for us to eat. Man, I'm starved."  Rosha sighed.

"You're hungry Dude.  You gotta be kidding.  look around you.... there's nothing here...I mean there is absolutely nothing here, where ever here is.... except us."  Jack coughed, his body beginning to struggle for air.

"We gotta find a way out of here.  Start looking for exit points Rosha. We need light. I can't see shit."  Jack coughed again, spitting up blood.

"Jack, calm down.... feel around for a wall, a door, anything that would get us out a here."  Rosha was doing his best to stay positive while protecting Jack from collasping again.

"The only thing here is emptiness. There's nothing but a floor."  Jack sighed.  "And the floor is moving, very slowly, taking us somewhere."

"This is crazy...nothing makes sense.  A floor, no light, no room, only a floor, which is moving us towards some unknown destination? Maybe?" Rosha was out of ideas.  Destiny had welcomed the two travelers to a dead-end, going nowhere, very slow.

"Ah....Rosha...this floor is tilting a bit.  Can you feel the difference?" Jack continued coughing.

"Yeah, I feel it...and I'm starting to lose my balance. I think we're about to slide off of this floor Jack."  Rosha sighed, trying to maintain his balance on a tilting floor which was now at a 45 Degree angle.

"Jack, I can't stop sliding.  There must be an edge to this floor. Hopefully, or we're gonna fly off into God knows where?"

The floor kept tilting until it was now in a 90-degree position, straight up and down.  Rosha and Jack were still affixed to this platform stressing their fingers and toes to stay attached to the floating floor.

"Dude, I can't stand erect without sliding loose from this platform.  The damn platform keeps rotating in a circle, throwing me off balance. Rosha, grab my arm, I'm starting to slide and I can't stop." Jack cried out for Rosha to save him.

Rasha grabbed jacks' arm to hold him firm against the floor. "Bro, how is this possible.  We should have fallen off of this flying platform minutes ago."  Jack continued coughing.

"There's nothing on this platform that makes sense.  I think we're revolving in a continuous circle...there's no end...." Rosha sighed. "Jack, your cough is getting worse."

"Yeah,yeah,yeah. We're not going anywhere.  So, how did we get here, where ever here is, and what's the hap's with this rotating platform or floating floor?"  Rosha was angry and confused. "We're not falling off of this floor, so we're somehow attached to it, right?"

"Maybe, maybe not. Maybe we're not even here on this floor, or platform.  Maybe this is all an illusion, another dream of mine with you and I in the Dream." Jack sighed, believing that the two new friends were morphed to this place because someone willed it to happen.

The question is, who is this someone, and why send Jack and Rosha to a deserted platform that doesn't exist anywhere in the World of reality, except inside this Black Void.

**CHAPTER 39**

**THE PLATFORM**

"Rosha, we're screwed.  This platform or floor is simply turning in circles, non-stop.  We can't see anything in the darkness of this place, and we can't find a way to return to Mother and the Menace.  We're stranded."  Jack shook his head in dismay.

"Your right.  We're stranded on a floor that isn't apart of anything.  So, the question is how to return to Mother and the Menace, if that's even important now."  Rosha sighed.

"It's important Rosha.  There has to be a key, or something, that will unlock us from this anomaly. Whatever dumped us here on this platform must have a key or a way to control it, right.  I mean, platforms just don't emerge outa nowhere.  This platform had to exist because someone made it, right?"

"Yeah.  That means someone knows how to control this thing. This person or thing must have morphed us to this platform, holding us prisoners in its Jail...kinda....right Jack?"

"This Platform has to of been created by someone.  It can't just be a wierd happening that popped up outa nowhere. It couldn't have just happened outa nowhere."  Rosha repeated himself.

"Or, an unknown creator planned to incarcerate us.  Someone wants to control us, but why?"  Jack frowned, looking at Rosha for answers.

So, here we are...alone in the darkness of hell, with no way to communicate to anyone, especially Mother.  It's an anomaly.  Someone wanted us out of the way, that someone could be the Black Menace or?"  Rosha shook his head in confusion.

"None of this shit that has happened to us can be real. It's too confining with no details as to who's pulling the strings." Jack looked at Rosha. "Is it possible that Mother or the Menace morphed us to this so-called Platform?"  Jack was playing Detective now, trying to solve the puzzle.

"Everything always comes back to WHO, WHAT AND WHY this has happened to us." Rosha sighed. "It's obvious that someone wants us out of the way, that's a given.  But, WHAT did we do to encourage this someone to send us to the  dark side of hell. Someone or something wants us to exist on this Platform, maybe forever."

"We're back to WHO....WHAT....AND WHY?" Jack noticed that the Platform they're standing on, was coming to a full stop.

"This is interesting.  The unknown benefactor or disruptor is controlling the Platform Rosha.  It's coming to a full stop.  That tells me we're being watched Rosha." Jack shook his head in the affirmative.

"You're right...the platform is no longer moving.  So, whoever is controlling this thing, has to be watching us, Jack." Rosha agreed with Jack's assessment of their situation.

"Whoa...we're moving again Rosha, hang on buddy, this thing is hauling ass."  Jack and Rosha laid down on the flat surface of the floor trying to keep from flying off the platform, into oblivion.

Time seemed to be constant, with no particular direction.  Then, the platform began traveling at light speed inside dark space.  The direction of the platform was in one direction only.  It's destination hopefully will reveal itself soon.

Rosha and Jack were compressed to the platform.  There was still nothing to hang onto.  The beginning and the ending were becoming one with the Universe.

"We're still blind, unable to see any kind of destination, location, or even a place of some kind." Rosha sighed, wanting an ending to their unwanted travels.

"Bro, we're being dragged through dark space on this flat piece of shit. Hang on Buddy."  Jack warned Rosha.

"Hang on to what?  It's all I can do to keep from flying off of this platform into the Dark side." Rosha sighed.

"There's nothing out here....in the dark, Jack. It's just us.  I can't tell if we're moving or if the dark matter around us is the thing that's moving and we're just inside of it?" Rosha sighed.

"I agree.  But why the game...someone or something is trying to fool us?" Jack sighed.  "Why us?"

"Dude, The Menace and Mother are the only two entities that seem to be controlling the Universe around us.  I think we're caught in the middle of their dispute, or fight."  Jack and Rosha were lying flat on the platform, hanging on for life.

"Mother....are you here?  The Menace searched for Mother, to continue the game.  "I am playing with your two boys, but not for much longer.  Show yourself or I let your two children become...well...you know what I mean, right?"  The Menace called out Mother to show herself IMMEDIATELY, or Jack and Rosha become casualties of War.

"You're brash,  and stupid.  You exist in this Cadaver body at my will.  You wish to disrupt my existence and that of my two Boys by Murdering us?"  Mother was angered, ready to compel the Menace to remove itself from the Cadaver Body, causing the Immediate death of the Menace.

"Wait, I am not interested in causing you or your Boys harm.  I simply wish to continue my existence in this body without favor.  My original body has turned to dust.  Please, forgive me.  I am not an adversary of yours.  I simple wish to meet with you, visibly....to thank you for your diligence in saving me from eternal death."  The Black Menace bowed to the power of MOTHER.

**CHAPTER 40**


**SAVING THE SEED**


"You are a liar and deserve what I am about to place on your head."
Mother was anxious to end the breath that extruded from the mouth of
the Menace.

"Okay...you got me...I really don't give a rats ass about you or your
Boys.  Let's get down to brass tacks."  The Menace was egging Mother
to listen to his rhetoric.

"Now it's my turn Menace.  I have one last Seed of life.  It can be used
to heal or to destroy.  It depends on who will receive the Seed."
Mother held the seed up for the Black Menace to see it.

"Mother, you tried that Seed crap on me at the Coroners Lab.  It didn't
work then and it won't work on me now.  So, shall I eliminate the
Platform that your two boys are suspended inside of? Or will you
confirm the Cadaver as mine, to do as I wish?"  The Menace looked at
Mother to test her willingness to save her two boys.

"Hum, you really are a Monster.  So, release Jack and Rosha from your
ridiculous Platform now, and we can settle the Cadaver situation
immediately."  Mother sighed.

"Yes, excellent. Okay then...the two boys are being released by one of my minions.  Now, let's get down to business."  The Menace was drooling with success over Mother, short lived as it may be.

"I want you and your clan of Seed Mongers to leave half of the Planet to me, the other half to whoever you wish.  That's number one.  Number two, the Cadaver is mine, permenantly and forever.  Number three, The Holy Rotunda is mine to exist, to rule over and to possess."  The Menace smiled, waiting impatiently for Mothers response.

"Well, I see you have been thinking about this situation you're involved with, for quite some time."  Mother watched the face of the Menace change from hope to Control.  Have Rosha and Jack Burton been released from the Platform?"

"Not yet, not until you agree in Blood, to hold your word as written and spoken on Parchment, for all to see your weakness."  The Menace sighed.

"Release Rosha and Jack Burton, then we talk, in blood if you wish."  Mother was baiting the Monster living inside a Cadaver's body with a mitigated verbal agreement.

"MOTHER, what's happening...we're back." Rosha sighed.  "We're no longer held prisoner on the Platform."

"Yes Rosha, but where is Jack Burton?" Mother looked at Rosha.  "So, you are still playing games Menace? This is not my Rosha.  It is a doubleganger.  You wish to play this game, then allow me to respond."

"Wait...I don't have a minion to free the two lads.  I... ah...was just trying to move this agreement ahead...faster than not.  I will release the two boys now, morphing them to your side."

"Do it...do it now Menace and save your existence from doom." Mother was angered, ready to dissolve the Menace one way or another.

Both Jack and Rosha appeared from the winds of time, standing before the Menace who had incarcerated them.

"There, I have kept my word, now it's your turn Mother?"  The Menace hissed at Mother. "Sign the Parchment with your blood, giving me power over the Cadaver, and control over half of the World."

"Your existence shall remain below the surface of the Planet, below the Crust of the Earth.  We shall exist above the Crust of Earth and the land existing top side."

"UMMM...we shall write on the parchment these terms and conditions, forthwith.  The existence below the Crust of the Earth shall be called HELL.  Your half of the World that exists above the Earth's crust shall be called......?" The Menace was curious and ready to fill in the blanks on the Parchment, ready for signature AND ready to rule as the King of the Underworld.

"The land above the Earth's Crust shall be referred to as, Heaven.  All innocents will exist in my World.  Those of evil who worship you shall exist in your world.  The two lands, lower and upper lands, shall never be breached by our side nor your side.  Agreed?"

"Yes, yes, Mother...I agree.  Now, let's complete the agreement, review it for errors or additions or subtractions.  We both sign the parchment, each with our everlasting Blood."  The Menace was excited to be called KING OF THE UNDERWORLD...

"The "SEED OF LIFE" shall reside in each and every body that exists topside.  Should a faction be created top side by your Minions, those evil and miserable souls will be returned to "Hell" and will belong to you.  Their everlasting souls shall remain in Hell, never to return topside unless they Repent.  Agreed?"

"I cannot agree with these terms in total. Each person or minion of mine...shall have the choice to exist where ever they wish."

"Then those minions of evil, your minions, shall be buried in the everlasting soil of Earth, their souls forgotten and lost over time, or sent back to you for prosecution.  Agreed?"  Mother looked at her adversary.

"Yes...yes agreed for now.  But don't think you can control my realm.  If you try, the Bargin is broken, the Parchment will burn in fire, and my wrath will consume you and your Seed to the end of time." The Black Menace was threatening Mother with the future of all existence.  The Black Menace was secretly smiling, knowing full well, the game was just beginning.


**CHAPTER 41**


**TO BE CONTINUED**

**BOOK 2**


**THE CONCLUSION**


**COMING SOON**

www.ingramcontent.com/pod-product-compliance
Lightning Source LLC
Chambersburg PA
CBHW081433250726
48662CB00009B/2774